THE DEFENSE SPEAKS
FOR HISTORY AND THE FUTURE

Yugoslav President SLOBODAN MILOSEVIC's
Opening Defense Statement

before the International Criminal Tribunal
for the Former Yugoslavia (ICTY) at The Hague,
August 31 – September 1, 2004

A Definitive Version of the ICTY Translation
Revised according to the Original Serbian Text
by Radmila Milentijevic
with the assistance of Milo Yelesiyevich

with an introduction by Ramsey Clark

International Action Center
New York

THE DEFENSE SPEAKS
for History and the Future

Copyright (c) 2006
ISBN 0-9747521-2-6

International Action Center
39 West 14th St, Suite 206
New York, NY, 10011
Phone: 212-633-6646
Website: www.iacenter.org
E-mail: iacenter@action-mail.org

We want to make this book available as widely as possible. Any properly attributed selection or part of a chapter within "fair-use" guidelines may be used without permission.

Copyright of Translation from Serbian Text by Dr. Radmila Milentijevic
Cover Design: Lal Roohk
Library of Congress Control Number: 2005909733

Cataloging Data:
THE DEFENSE SPEAKS: for History and the Future; Slobodan Milosevic's Opening Defense Statement before the International Criminal Tribunal for the Former Yugoslavia (ICTY) at The Hague, August 31 - September 1, 2004, translation by Rudmila Milentijevic.
Introduction by Ramsey Clark
120 pp
Includes index.
ISBN 0-9747521-2-6 (pb : alk.paper)

1. Yugoslavia-History-1992- 2. North Atlantic Treaty Organization-Armed Forces-Yugoslavia. 3. Kosovo (Serbia)-History-Civil War, 1998-Participation, American. Operation Allied Force, 1999. 5. International Tribunal for the Prosecution of Persons Responsible for Serious Violations of International Humanitarian Law Committed in the Territory of the Former Yugoslavia since 1991. 6. United States-Foreign Relations-Yugoslavia. 7. Yugoslavia--Foreign Relations-United States. I.Title: THE DEFENSE SPEAKS: for History and the Future. II.Milosevich, Slobodan. III.Clark, Ramsey.

DR1319 .D23 2006
949.7-dc21 2005909733

TABLE OF CONTENTS

Chronology	4
Preface — For History and the Future, Today	**5**
by John Catalinotto and Sara Flounders	
Acknowledgements	7
Introduction — Ramsey Clark's Letter to UN Secretary General Kofi Annan	9
President Milosevic's Opening Defense Speech	**17**
The First Day — August 31, 2004	17
The Outbreak of Hostilities	19
Erroneous Recognition	27
The Illegitimacy of the Tribunal	28
Germany's Role	31
The Myth of "Greater Serbia"	36
The Destruction of Yugoslavia	42
The Role of the Vatican	44
The Role of the United States	48
The Role of the International Community	50
Illegal Secessions	54
The Drama of Kosovo	56
Albanian Separatism	61
Acts of Terrorism Committed by the KLA	64
American Intervention	69
The Aggression against Yugoslavia	73
Ruins and Devastation	78
The Second Day — September 1, 2004	**81**
Croatian Separatism	83
The Muslims in Bosnia	89
The Real Perpetrators	95
False Witnesses	98
Serbian Pluralism	100
Endnotes	105
Appendices	
Experts in International Law Back Milosevic Defense	107
Artists Appeal for Milosevic	109
Imposition of Counsel on Slobodan Milosevic Threatens the Future of International Law and the Life of the Defendant	111
Index	115

Chronology

June 25, 1991 - Slovenia and Croatia unilaterally secede from the Yugoslav Federation; Germany immediately recognizes secession, and with U.S. encourages political leaders of Bosnia-Hercegovina to secede, leading to brutal civil war.

March 19, 1992 - U.S. sabotages accord Bosnian Muslims, Croats and Serbs reach in Lisbon for a unified state. Civil war continues three more years.

Feb 22, 1993 - At U.S. Secretary of State Madeleine Albright's insistence, the International Criminal Tribunal on the Former Yugoslavia (ICTY) is established in The Hague to try Balkans politicians, especially Serbs.

Aug 4, 1995 - Croatian military, led by future head of Kosovo Liberation Army (KLA) Brig. Gen. Agim Ceko, launches "Operation Storm" with U.S. military backing, driving 300,000 ethnic Serbs from Krajina region.

Nov 21, 1995 - President Milosevic and presidents of Bosnia and Croatia initial Dayton Peace Accords in Paris. U.S./NATO occupation begins; troops are still there in 2005.

Jan. 15, 1999 - With help from U.S. diplomat William Walker, KLA disguises military battle in town of Racak, Kosovo, as massacre of civilians. U.S. uses staged event to justify NATO military intervention.

March 1999 - In Rambouillet, France, U.S. proposal used to demand Yugoslavia give NATO total power as occupation force in Kosovo and all Yugoslavia, forces Yugoslav refusal and serves as pretext for war.

March 24, 1999 - U.S./NATO planes begin 78 days systematic bombing of Serbia, including the province of Kosovo. Bombs destroy only 14 tanks, but hit 480 schools and 33 hospitals, chemical plants along with vital civilian infrastructure.

May 27, 1999 - In the midst of bombing, NATO succeeds in getting the ICTY to announce indictment of President Milosevic on trumped-up war crimes charges regarding Kosovo.

June 10, 1999 - After June 3 ceasefire, NATO troops begin occupation of Kosovo. Under KLA rule, expulsion of some 300,000 Serbs, Roma and other peoples of mixed nationalities also begins.

Nov 10, 1999 - Carla Del Ponte, chief prosecutor for UN War Crimes announces that UN war crimes investigators found no mass graves in Kosovo.

Sept 24, 2000 - Milosevic's Socialist Party of Serbia (SPS) comes in second in election to Vojislav Kostunica, head of the Democratic Opposition of Serbia (DOS), a coalition cobbled together with U.S. money and advisers.

Oct 5, 2000 - To avoid a run off election, DOS and other anti-SPS forces make a coup with U.S. support and depose President Milosevic.

March 31, 2001 - President Milosevic arrested to comply with U.S. deadline

June 28, 2001 - Milosevic illegally turned over to NATO authorities on St. Vitus Day and taken to Scheveningen Prison in the Netherlands to stand trial before ICTY on charges of war crimes. Charges later broadened to include alleged crimes regarding Croatia and Bosnia, in attempt to make "trial of the century."

Feb. 12, 2002 - Trial begins. President Milosevic defends self, opens trial with powerful statement accusing U.S. and NATO forces of war crimes.

Feb. 24, 2004 - prosecution ends its case after two years.

PREFACE
For history and the future — and for today

"For history and the future," is how we described the impact of President Slobodan Milosevic's opening defense speech. And this description is true. But as we will show below, it is also for today.

For history, because the coalition of NATO powers led by the United States that imposed 10 years of intervention and 78 days of horrific bombing on the Yugoslav peoples, would also like to have complete control of the history of these events, just as they had monopoly control of the media reports from the Balkans during that period. But President Milosevic has taken that monopoly away from them. By his courageous defense at the illegal "trial" at The Hague, he has established an historical record. His defense speech of August 31-September 1, 2004, is a clear and concise history of the period his country was under attack from the imperialist U.S. and Western Europe, especially Germany.

For the future, because the current-day situation in the Balkans, with countries torn into tiny pieces representing every division of religion, language and customs so that the United States and Western Europe can dominate them militarily, economically and diplomatically, can not endure. An educated and skilled population will not allow itself to be treated forever as a subject people. Resistance is inevitable, and this resistance will look to the record of the kangaroo court where President Milosevic held up his head, the courage of the Serb people and of all the peoples of the Balkans while combating the most unreasonable odds.

History and the future are important. But we live in the now. And now is when this book can begin to have its most telling effect. One of the tragedies of the 1999 war on Yugoslavia was that Washington and Berlin were able to impose their biased view of the Serbian people in general and of President Milosevic in particular on their home populations. Not only were the mass of uninvolved people deceived, even the usually more progressive sectors, especially in the United States, were duped into believing that somehow an intervention from the Pentagon and the Bundeswehr could somehow serve the cause of "human rights."

Now the sorry attempt of the Bush administration to lie its way into an aggressive war against Iraq, and the exposure of those lies during a prolonged armed resistance from the Iraqi people has awaked millions to the tactics coming out of Washington. The credibility of the White House has been broken, and rightfully so. The whole world now knows that the Bush administration's claim about Iraq's "weapons of mass destruction" was a Big Lie, an intentional fraud used to justify a criminal war.

In a similar way, the endlessly repeated claims of Serbian massacres of 100,000 to 500,000 people, the claims there were hundreds of mass graves in Kosovo were used to justify 78 days of U.S./NATO bombing and the continuing occupation. Everyone heard those claims. But many fewer are aware that two months after the bombing ended, the UN sent to Kosovo forensic teams from 17 countries, including U.S., Britain, France, Spain and Germany, to gather the evidence of mass graves. They dug all over and found not one mass grave in all of Kosovo. Yet President Milosevic was kidnapped and brought to The Hague to stand trial for war crimes before a Tribunal the U.S. and NATO established. Those who ordered the bombing and destruction sit in judgment.

With millions, maybe tens of millions of people now questioning authority, will it be possible to convince them also to review and rethink their earlier conclusions about the war on Yugoslavia? To show them that the Big Lie didn't end with Hitler and restart only with Bush? We in the International Action Center believe this is possible, and that is why we are publishing the defense speech of President Milosevic. But to be successful in the now will take the help of those who read these words and read the president's speech and are convinced of the truth. And this success will depend on getting the book around to more and more people, of getting it into libraries, into universities, and into the hands of those opinion makers who earlier were deceived by the lies of the Clinton administration and the corporate media on two continents.

This will be the fourth book the IAC has published exposing U.S. aims in the Balkans. They accompany the other books and videos the IAC produced, the internet campaigns and massive demonstrations we have mobilized to stand against a policy of endless war, racism and corporate greed that endangers all of us, our history, our future, our today.

John Catalinotto and Sara Flounders,
for the *International Action Center*, November 2005

Acknowledgments

This book, as with all the books published by the International Action Center has been a collective and volunteer effort. Many people have offered their time and considerable talents.

The French version of President Milosevic's defense speech was seen for the first time at a February 2005 meeting in The Hague, of the International Committee for the Defense of Slobodan Milosevic. It inspired us to publish an English version of this historic summation of the Yugoslav wars by a defendant standing in the dock accusing his accusers. Knowing that the official English translation was an awkward, hasty court translation that was questionable at best, we started by checking the French version against the English version. Jovana Ruzicic, a Serb student studying in the U.S., offered to check the translation against President Milosevic's original Serbian speech. What made this especially encouraging was that, as a teenager Jovana had considered herself an opponent of President Milosevic, but had read the International Action Center's earlier book "Hidden Agenda – U.S.-NATO Takeover of Yugoslavia" in a school library and now wanted to help his defense.

This got us underway, but the effort took a big leap forward when writer and filmmaker Milo Yelesijevich offered to edit, proof and lay out the text. We were confident that we would have a serious, historically accurate translation when The City College of The City University of New York Professor Emeritus Radmila Milentijevic, once a member of President Milosevic's cabinet, went over the Serbian original from beginning to end, retranslating where necessary (and much was necessary) and removing the many distortions from the numerous court translators at the Hague.

There are many additional steps in publishing a book. Lal Roohk designed the front and back cover, Ellen Catalinotto, Paddy Colligan and G. Dunkel proofread the results. Prof. Barry Lituchy, Heather Cottin, composer Milos Raickovich and writer Nadja Tesich helped organize the contacts needed to make the book a success. We also want to thank the IAC staff – Carol Holland, Marie Jay, William Mason, Henri Nereaux and Walter Williams – for providing the daily organizational assistance at the office. But without financial assistance, none of this work could have borne fruit.

ACKNOWLEDGMENTS TO DONORS

We thank all of those whose commitment to getting this book produced and out into public view showed in their generous financial support for its publication.

Those named below and the many who gave anonymously have demonstrated their steadfastness on this issue and shown their determination to get out the truth about very a very important, yet often hidden subject in the U.S. media and history books.

Their support for the projects that produced this book and the two prior Works—that tell the real story of the U.S. and NATO roles in the Balkans in recent history and up to the current day—is a major contribution to not only anti-war activists and movements in the U.S., but around the world.

Our gratitude goes to B.M. Vukovich for his commitment to and support for the publication of this historic book.

We recognize and thank the following individuals:

Benefactors: John Martjak, Kosa Martjak, Radmila Milentijevic, Tijana Nikov, Van Nikov, Phylis Lucero, Nick Pavlica, Mihailo Petrovic, M.D.

Supporters: Bogdan Baishanski, Olga Emmel, Mary Kral, Irene R. Leiby,

Donors: Dusica Babovic, Allan Billings, Conrad Brenner, John Catalinotto, Timothy Connelly, Alvin and Chelle Dorfman, George V. Fatsi, Sara Flounders, Dr. Jovan Jovanovic, Steffan Manno, James Mendieta, Milos Raickovich, Bill Moore, Edith Oxfeld, Branislava Stefanovic, Traian Stoianovich, Nadja Tesich, Andrea B. Vider-Myers, Milo Yelesiyevich, Joe Yuskaitis

Friends: Aleksandar Ajdukovic, Carl Boggs, Frank R. Bubic, Arthur Carney, Lillian Carney, Jeanne Sritesic Cecil, Heather Cottin, Biljana Djelevich, Vojislav Dosenovich, Hester Eisenstein, Beatrice Eisman, David M. Graybeal, Vaughn Guloyan, Roger D. Harris, Edward Hoffmans, Rev. William J. Hutton, Tika Jankovic, VDK (CA), Milan Knezovich, V. Rev. Fr. Djuro G. Krosnjar, Barry Lituchy, Joan Mathews, Moon and River Cafe (Schenectady, NY), Ivanka Ostojic, Alice O. Ritter, Leonard D. Sanford, Jr., Mirjana Sasich, Marjorie Smith, Roger S. Wilson

Ramsey Clark's Letter to Kofi Annan

February 12, 2004

Re: The Trial of Slobodan Milosevic, Former President of the Federal Republic of Yugoslavia Before the International Criminal Tribunal for the Former Yugoslavia

Dear Secretary General Annan,

The Prosecution of the former President of the Federal Republic of Yugoslavia is scheduled to end its presentation of evidence to the International Criminal Tribunal for the Former Yugoslavia (ICTY) on February 19, 2004, more than two years after its first witness testified.*

Over 500,000 pages of documents and 5,000 videocassettes have been placed in evidence. There have been some 300 trial days. More than 200 witnesses have testified. The trial transcript is near 33,000 pages.

The Prosecution has failed to present significant or compelling evidence of any criminal act or intention of President Milosevic. In the absence of incriminating evidence, the Prosecution apparently hoped to create a record so massive that it would be years, if the effort was ever made, before scholars could examine and analyze the evidence to determine whether it supported a conviction.

Meanwhile the spectacle of this huge onslaught by an enormous prosecution support team with vast resources pitted against a single man, defending himself, cut off from all effective assistance, his supporters under attack everywhere and his health slipping away from the constant strain, portrays the essence of unfairness, of persecution.

In contrast, the Prosecution of the "first trial in history for crimes against the peace of the world" at Nuremberg began November 20, 1945 against 19 accused and ended just over three months later on March 4, 1946 after four nations presented evidence. In his opening, Chief Prosecutor Robert H. Jackson observed

> There is a dramatic disparity between the circumstances of the accusers and the accused that might discredit our work if we should falter, in even minor matters, in being fair and temperate. ... We must never forget that the record on which we judge these defendants is the record on which history will judge us tomorrow. To pass these defendants a poisoned chalice is to put it to our lips as well.

The Prosecution began its investigation of President Milosevic under Richard Goldstone of South Africa in October 1994. When he left office in December 1996 he had found no evidence to support an indictment. His successor, Louise Arbour of Canada, continued the investigation without formal action until late May 1999 when President Milosevic was first indicted for acts allegedly committed earlier in 1999.

The indictment came during the heavy U.S./NATO bombing of all Serbia including Kosovo, a war of aggression. It had killed civilians throughout Serbia and destroyed property costing billions of dollars to replace. It had destroyed President Milosevic's home in Belgrade in an assassination attempt on April 22, 1999. The Chinese Embassy in Belgrade had been bombed on May 7, 1999. Depleted uranium, cluster bombs and super bombs had targeted civilians and civilian facilities. Hundreds of civilian facilities were destroyed and civilians killed from Nova Sad to Nis to Pristina.

The initial indictment made no allegations of any crimes in Croatia, or Bosnia. It dealt exclusively with alleged acts by Serb forces in Kosovo in 1999. All of Serbia, including Kosovo, remained under heavy U.S./NATO bombardment at the time of the indictment. There were no U.S., or NATO forces, or ICTY investigators in Kosovo. Investigation was impossible. The indictment was purely a political act to demonize President Milosevic and Serbia and justify U.S. and NATO bombing of Serbia which was itself criminal and in violation of the U.N. and NATO Charters.

As U.S. Ambassador to the U.N., Madeleine Albright led the U.S. effort to cause the Security Council to create the ICTY. Later she wrote in her memoir that while she was U.S. Secretary of State she had sought removal of President Milosevic from office for years:

> With colleagues Joschka Fischer and others, I urged Serb opposition leaders to build a real political organization and focus on pushing Milosevic out... In public remarks I said repeatedly that the United States wanted Milosevic "out of power, out of Serbia, and in the custody of the war crimes tribunal."

President Milosevic was indicted and is on trial because he intended and acted to protect and preserve Yugoslavia, a federation that was essential to peace in the Balkans. Powerful foreign interests, supporting nationalist and ethnic groups and business interests within the several republics of Yugoslavia, were, for their various reasons, determined to dismember Yugoslavia. Foremost among these was the United States. Germany played a major role. Later NATO lent its name to the effort in violation of its own Charter. The violence that followed was foreseeable and tragic.

Throughout there was no more conciliatory leader than President Milosevic who avoided all out war as Slovenia, Croatia, Bosnia and Macedonia seceded from the Federal Republic. For his later defense of Yugoslavia, reduced to Serbia and Montenegro, he will be remembered primarily for his compromises at Dayton, Ohio and, later, to end the brutal U.S. bombing of Serbia from March to June 1999. His conduct intended peace and the survival of a core federation of southern Slavs which in a better day might seed a broader federation of Balkan states which is essential to peace, political independence and economic viability in the region. The U.S. and others intended otherwise.

The consequences have been disastrous for each of the former states of the federal republic. Today there is economic intervention and stagnation, political unrest, public dissatisfaction and growing threats of violence in former Yugoslavia. The U.S. is courting Croatia for membership in NATO as the base for European forces to control the region and maintain its division. Croatia has sent a small military unit to assist NATO in Afghanistan and is being pressured to send troops to Iraq, thereby continuing its confrontations with Muslim peoples in Croatian and Bosnia. U.S. Secretary of Defense Rumsfeld, met with the nationalist leadership of Croatia, including the President and Prime Minister, on February 8, 2004. He proclaimed "I look forward to the day when Croatia becomes a part" of NATO.

The former President of Yugoslavia is on trial for defending Yugoslavia in a court the Security Council had no power to create. In contrast, the President of the United States, who has openly and notoriously committed war of aggression, "the supreme international crime", against a defenseless Iraq killing tens of thousands of people, spreading violence there and elsewhere, faces no charges. President Bush continues to threaten unilateral wars of aggression and presses for U.S. development of a new generation of nuclear weapons, tactical nuclear bombs, after invading Iraq on the fabricated claim it was a threat to the U.S. and possessed weapons of mass destruction. This can happen only because power, not principle, still prevails.

The United Nations cannot hope to end the scourge of war until it finds the will to outface power and stands united for the principles of peace. What better evidence is needed of U.S. intention to stand above the law and rule by force than the extensive U.S. efforts to destroy the International Criminal Court and coerce bilateral treaties in which nations agree not to surrender U.S. citizens to the ICC. Compound this obstruction of justice with the June 30, 2002 statement of the U.S. Permanent Representative to the U.N., Ambassador John Negroponte, demanding immunity for the U.S. from foreign prosecution, to which the Security Council submitted. Negroponte threatened that the U.S. would veto a pending Security Council resolution to renew the U.N. peacekeeping mission in Bosnia-Herzegovina, unless the Security Council provided immunity, that is impunity, for personnel contributed to Security Council authorized peace keeping missions. The purpose was to place U.S. personnel and U.S. surrogates above the law while U.S. enemies are victims of discriminatory prosecution in illegal courts.

The ICTY and other *ad hoc* criminal tribunals created by the Security Council are illegal because the Charter of the United Nations does not empower the Security Council to create any criminal court. The language of the Charter is clear. Had such power been placed in the Charter in 1945 there would be no U.N. None of the five powers made permanent members of the Security Council in the Charter would have agreed to submit to a U.N. criminal report.

The ICC was created by treaty, recognizing the U.N. had no power without amendment of its Charter to create such a court. Creation of the ICC should preclude creation of any additional criminal tribunals and calls for the abolition of those that exist. They were created to serve geo political ambitions of the U.S. The issue is of the highest importance. It determines whether the Security Council itself is above the Charter and the rule of law.

The *ad hoc* criminal tribunals are inherently discriminatory, evading the principles of equality in the administration of justice. The discrimination is intended to destroy enemies. The

International Criminal Tribunal of Rwanda has not indicted a single Tutsi after nine years, though Faustin Twagirimungu, the first Prime Minister under the Tutsi RPF government in 1994 and 1995, testified before it that he believed more Hutu's than Tutsi's were killed in Rwanda in the tragic violence of 1994. Hundreds of thousands of Hutu's were slaughtered later in Zaire, now the Democratic Republic of Congo, and remain endangered today. The ICTR is an instrumentality for U.S. support of Tutsi control in Uganda, Rwanda, Burundi, and for a time and perhaps again, the Democratic Republic of Congo.

ICTY prosecutions are overwhelmingly against Serbs and only Serb leaders have been indicted by it, including not only President Milosevic and Serb leadership, but Serb leaders in Srpska, the segregated Serb part of Bosnia.

As the prosecution of the former President of Yugoslavia draws to a close his health is seriously impaired and has become life threatening. Hearings were cancelled last week because he was too ill to participate, but the Tribunal added onerous hours of hearings for the two final weeks of the prosecution case. Only yesterday the Tribunal was forced to reduce the hearings to half days because of a medical report on President Milosevic prepared by court appointed doctors. President Milosevic has been kept in total isolation for months during the period he headed the socialist party's ticket in parliamentary elections and when his party joined the coalition which elected the new speaker of the Parliament last week. Earlier this week the Tribunal extended his isolation for another month because of political events in Serbia.

President Milosevic, imprisoned, his health dangerously impaired, defending himself alone in the courtroom, has been given less than three months to prepare his defense to more than two years of evidence before the defense presentation is scheduled to begin in May. These most recent actions of the Tribunal are representative of the gross consistent unfairness of the proceedings during the years of President Milosevic imprisonment and the prosecution case against him.

To properly prepare the defense, it will be necessary to secure and review tens of thousands of documents, find and interview hundreds of potential witnesses and organize the evidence into a coherent and effective presentation.

The United Nations must take the following acts in the interest of simple justice, to right former wrongs, to assess the legality and fairness of a court it created and to maintain credibility in the eyes of the Peoples of the United Nations:

1. **Declare a moratorium on all proceedings in all U.N.** *ad hoc* **criminal tribunals for a period of at least six months and for such additional periods as may prove necessary for the United Nations to:**

   A. **Create a Commission of international public law scholars and historians to examine the precedents, the drafting, language and intention of the Charter of the United Nations to determine whether the Charter empowers the Security Council to create any criminal tribunal and, if so, the basis, authority and scope of such power, or refer the issue to the International Court of Justice for decision.**

   B. **Create a commission of international criminal law scholars to review the trial proceedings in the case against President Milosevic to determine whether legal errors, violations of due process of law, or unfairness in the conduct of the trial compel dismissal of the proceedings, and whether the evidence presented by the prosecution against former President Milosevic to is sufficient under international law, before any defense is presented, to support and justify continuation of the trial.**

   C. **Provide former President Milosevic with funds to retain advisory counsel, investigators, researchers, document examiners and other experts sufficient to effectively respond to the evidence presented against him and assure the time required to complete the task before any further trial proceedings resume, such efforts being essential even if the court is abolished, or the prosecution has been dismissed in order to help establish historic fact for future peace.**

D. Provide funds to secure independent medical diagnoses, treatment and care for former President Milosevic in facilities in Serbia.

> Respectfully submitted,
> Ramsey Clark

The identical letter has been sent to:
—Members of the UN Security Council
—The President of the UN General Assembly
—The Secretary General of the UN
—The President of the United States
—The International Criminal Tribunal for Former Yugoslavia

---

* Submitted with this letter is a 31-page document entitled *Divide and Conquer* which supports in greater detail the facts, law and arguments set forth and the relief requested herein. Its Table of Contents provides a ready reference to the pages where subject matters of particular interest will be found.

Available at:
    www.iacenter.org
    www.icdsm.org

The Opening Defense Statement of
PRESIDENT SLOBODAN MILOSEVIC

Before the International Criminal Tribunal for the Former Yugoslavia (ICTY) in The Hague, August 31–September 1, 2004

THE FIRST DAY — TUESDAY AUGUST 31, 2004.

[Defense Opening Statement]

[Open Session]

——Upon commencing at 9:02 a.m.

JUDGE PATRICK ROBINSON: Mr. Milosevic, you may proceed with your opening statement.

PRESIDENT SLOBODAN MILOSEVIC: Mr. Robinson, for my opening statement, I would need tomorrow as well. I would like to note that the other side had three days, so I expect you to be so kind as to make today and tomorrow available to me as well.

May I start now?

JUDGE PATRICK ROBINSON: Mr. Milosevic, this is your third bite at the proverbial cherry. In response to the Prosecution's opening on the Kosovo part of the indictment, you were allowed eight hours, two days. And in response to the Prosecution's opening on the Bosnian and Croatian indictment you were allowed three and a half hours. This is your third bite. Please proceed.

PRESIDENT SLOBODAN MILOSEVIC: Mr. Robinson, you personally, you yourself said that I have the right to a statement and to opening arguments. What I made were statements, not an opening argument. Therefore, bear this in mind and consider my request for additional time.

JUDGE PATRICK ROBINSON: Please proceed, Mr. Milosevic.

PRESIDENT SLOBODAN MILOSEVIC: Thank you, Mr. Robinson.
  An untruthful, distorted picture of what happened in the territory of the former Yugoslavia was created in international public opinion over a long period of time with clear political intentions. These

charges represent an unscrupulous manipulation of lies, a perversion of law, a defeat of morals, and an extreme distortion of history. Everything has been turned upside down in order to shield from responsibility those who are truly responsible for the tragic events, to render the wrong judgments and to draw the wrong conclusions about the nature and background of the war against Yugoslavia.

There is one fundamental historical fact from which it is necessary to proceed when seeking to understand what happened and what led to everything that occurred in the territory of Yugoslavia from 1991 until the present day. And this is the violent destruction of a European state, Yugoslavia, which was itself derived from the Serbian state, the only ally the democratic world had in this area over the past two centuries. There is no doubt that this fundamental historical fact is going to leave an imprint on European history in times to come.

A multi-ethnic, multi-cultural, multi-confessional state was destroyed, a state that had its own historic and international legitimacy. Ethnically pure mini nation-states were established on its territory, according to the Diktat of Germany and the Vatican, assisted by the United States and the European Community. The state that was destroyed had been recognized by all international organizations starting with the first Postal Union in 1884, through the League of Nations, international labor organizations, the United Nations, the World Bank, the International Monetary Fund, and all the remaining specialized agencies of the United Nations, as well as the Organization for Security and Cooperation in Europe.

Who was behind this catastrophe — the destruction of a sovereign state — that, according to the principles of [the] Nuremberg [War Crimes Tribunal], constitutes the gravest of international crimes, the crime against peace? Who is responsible for the outbreak of a war in which tens of thousands of civilians were killed, hundreds of thousands of people were maimed, and more than a million people, mostly Serbs, were expelled or forced to flee their homes? The material damage is practically impossible to calculate and is in the hundreds of billions of dollars. This is not to speak of the ecological disaster involved.

The international community will have to face up to the truth. And the problem of responsibility is all the greater because not only was a state destroyed but the legal system of the United Nations was also destroyed, as well as the body of moral principles upon which world civilization is based. In addition, never in history has a state disappeared by chance.

The official rhetoric about the events on Yugoslavia's soil, from the inception of the crisis to the present day, which has even been adopted by this so-called Tribunal, dissolves when confronted with the naked facts. The fact is that Yugoslavia did not fall apart nor did it mysteriously disappear into thin air, as Mr. Robert Badinter[1] tried to explain, resorting to some kind of legal metaphysics. This country was violently destroyed according to a plan, and by a war, which continues to be waged, and in which a series of war crimes were committed.

A prominent American theoretician, Steven John Stedman, rightly noted in 1993 in the periodical *Foreign Affairs* that at the beginning of the war, and I quote: "[T]here was no Slovenia ... but a state called Yugoslavia," whose Presidency at this most critical time was headed by a representative from Croatia, Stjepan Mesic, whose Prime Minister was also from Croatia — Ante Markovic, as well as the Minister of Foreign Affairs — Budimir Loncar. As for the upper echelons of the military (of which we were advised in this court), there were only two Serbs among the top sixteen generals, the majority of whom were Croats, Slovenes and other nationalities.

This state had strong and well-organized armed forces that were in a position to keep the conflict under control and prevent catastrophe from taking place. However, the government let paramilitary formations, arms smugglers, criminals, even the narco Mafia (if we look at the end of this entire process in Kosovo) have their way. And the government acted in concert with the European Community, notably Germany and the Vatican.

The European Community insisted, even by the end of June 1991, that the legitimate army remain in its barracks and avoid any action whatsoever, thereby willfully transforming the army into detainees in their own country; and this, in turn, gave paramilitary forces room to maneuver with armed secessionist actions. Military actions started with the secession of Slovenia in 1991.

The Outbreak of Hostilities

In June 1991, Slovenian military formations killed JNA[2] soldiers who were securing the borders of Austria and Italy without cause and in cold blood, and took over the border posts. From the point of view of the constitution of Yugoslavia, the UN Charter, and general legal principles recognized by civilized nations, this was a classic example of an armed rebellion against the state. Therefore, the state was duty-bound to take all necessary measures in order to restore law and order. We know that, acting on the orders of the federal Prime Minister, Ante Markovic, the commander of the Fifth Army, a Slovenian, General Konrad Kolsek, informed the government of Slovenia that the Yugoslav People's Army would retake control of the border and that this task would be carried out.

The Slovenian leadership, instead of making it possible to carry out these decisions of the federal authorities peacefully, responded that it was taking up that challenge and would resort to force in order to oppose it, which they did. Slovenia launched an armed assault with its paramilitary forces, which numbered thirty-six thousand illegally armed men at the time. All of them knew full well that the Yugoslav army, educated in the spirit of brotherhood and unity, would not shoot Slovenes, whom they considered their own citizens, which resulted in the killing of the JNA soldiers, clearly a premeditated crime rather than an act of war.

Grave war crimes were committed and not even military medical institutions were spared. The Troika of the European Community toured the area and described the dramatic situation. The list of crimes is long and there is also film material documenting the crimes committed by Slovenian paramilitary forces. This footage was shot by an Austrian TV company. Due to the time constraints that you have imposed upon me, I cannot play these tapes now, but I am going to call certain witnesses to the stand and show these tapes later.

On July 10, 1991, the European parliament passed a resolution that condemned neither the rebels nor the secessionists but the sole legal armed force, the Yugoslav People's Army. An inversion of the executioner and the victim was carried out that was wholeheartedly supported by the American and European media, which had placed themselves in the service of the war and had become its driving force. I am pointing this out because it has been said ever since, time and again, that this is what happened in the former Yugoslavia, and this is a formula that has always been resorted to.

In Croatia, crimes against Serbs began even earlier, even before secession had been declared, by using the same methods and [targeting] the same areas where Ustasha formations in the so-called Independent State of Croatia initiated genocide against the Serbian people in 1941.

World renowned experts who studied genocide as it occurred in different times and different places, for example, Leo Cooper, Peter Drost, Ted Gertz, Louis Horowitz, George Cram and others, reached the same conclusion: that genocide against a people can occur only once. Any further attempt would result in civil war. And this thesis was confirmed in Croatia.

The genocide against the Serbs in Croatia in 1941 started with drawing up lists and calling upon groups ostensibly "for the purpose of giving them information." However, instead of being given information, Serbs were killed on the spot or sent off to concentration camps. This time, when similar calls and similar attempts were made, the Serbs answered with resistance, because they realized that they had been manipulated by politicians, who, until that very moment, had defended the ideals of brotherhood and unity but were now calling for war in the name of national ideals.

Old Ustasha formulas and symbols were repackaged with slightly different wrapping and circulated. Laws were quickly passed that stripped the Serbs of their status as a constituent people. Without any outside orders, without any support from Belgrade, without any protection from the JNA, which was still isolated in its barracks, the Serbs in Krajina were not going to submit to another genocide and were prepared to die fighting.

Armed groups were operating in Croatia long before its secession in 1991. The so-called Voluntary People's Protection Forces were operating within the HDZ[3] under various names, such as "Zebra," "Black Legion," "Vukovar Wolves," etc. In Zagreb on May 28, a military parade was organized — one whole month before secession — where arms that came primarily from Germany were exhibited.

These were psychological preparations for what was to follow. Groups of Croatian paramilitary forces were transferred to Bosnia at that time because President Tudjman had announced that he was going to restore Croatia's borders on the Drina River. Armed paramilitary forces in Croatia started a war by implementing frontal attacks following the decision to withdraw the JNA from Slovenia and Croatia on July 18, 1991. From July 20 to August 4, there were seventy-five attacks against units of the JNA, twenty-three on military barracks and thirteen on military aircraft; all of these attacks utilized the most modern weapons from NATO's arsenal. Serbian houses were set on fire and the initial individual crimes against Serbs escalated to mass liquidations.

JUDGE PATRICK ROBINSON: Mr. Milosevic, the interpreters are asking you to speak slowly, more slowly.

PRESIDENT SLOBODAN MILOSEVIC: They could have said that to me.

Sixty-five Serbs were slaughtered in a cornfield near the village of Jankovac. All of them have been identified. Twenty-five were killed in the village of Svinjarevo, and so on. Entire villages in the area of Papuk and Slunj were razed. The most widespread form of terror against the Serbian people was forcible expulsions, demonstrating the strongest link between 1941 and 1991.

These activities began in Western Slavonia immediately after the HDZ won elections there, creating a psychosis of fear to induce people to leave. Various methods were used. Serbian children were mocked in school. People were brought into police stations. Telephones were turned off. There were mass dismissals of Serbs from work. Their houses were blown up. On October 28, 1991, the Crisis Staff in Slavonska Pozega issued an order for the eviction of Serbs from 24 villages: Oblakovac, Orijaca, Slatina and others, within a period of forty-eight hours. This order was broadcast on the radio and published in the press. Those who refused to comply were taken to concentration camps. A large-scale exodus of Serbs in the areas of Podravska Slatina and Daruvar began. 193 Serbian villages were ethnically cleansed between July 1991 and July 1992. Credible documents pertaining to all this have been submitted to the European Union.

Warlike actions then spread to the territory of Bosnia and Herzegovina. The ideological foundations had already been laid in 1970 with the publication of Alija Izetbegovic's *The Islamic Declaration*, as a secret political program. Later, in 1984, another book by the same author, *Islam Between East and West,* was published, and then *The Islamic Declaration* was republished in 1990. It is well known that it states: "There can be neither peace nor coexistence between the Islamic faith and non-Islamic faiths," and this is repeated in the book many times.

At a session of the Bosnia-Herzegovina Assembly held on December 21, 1991, Izetbegovic stated: "I am prepared to sacrifice peace for a sovereign Bosnia and Herzegovina."

A mass mobilization, based on the principles of *The Islamic Declaration*, was carried out and a civil war broke out with abundant financial aid arriving from Saudi Arabia, Iran, and other Islamic countries. The arrival of large numbers of mujahedin followed.

At the Sixth Summit of the Organization of the Islamic Conference, which was held December 9–12, 1991, before Bosnia and Herzegovina was recognized and before the war burst into a total conflagration, support was given to fellow Muslims and to their struggle for the creation of the first Islamic state in Europe, even though Bosnia and Herzegovina does not have a majority Muslim population. Alija Izetbegovic was honored at the Conference and received substantial financial aid.

Bosnia-Herzegovina was one of the main topics at the extraordinary meeting of ministers at the Islamic Conference held in Jeddah on December 1 and 2, 1992. This time, the ministers extended their concerns to two areas in Serbia: Kosovo and the district of Raska, or, as they call it, Sandzak. The first "holy warriors," the mujahedin, arrived from Afghanistan, Lebanon, Morocco and Pakistan, armed with weapons that had been sent by the CIA to Afghan rebels. A group of 400 Hezbollah arrived in Sarajevo as military instructors.

Tudjman and Izetbegovic, the two leaders of the rebel paramilitary forces, who were following the World War II tradition of joint actions by military forces under the auspices of Nazi Germany against the democratic coalition to which Yugoslavia then belonged, signed an agreement in Zagreb, which stipulated, among other things, that the armed forces of the Croatian Defense Council would be part of the unified armed forces of Bosnia-Herzegovina. This was followed by the expulsion of Serbs from areas under the control of Muslim forces. Tens of thousands of people were expelled from Mostar, two and a half thousand from Gorazde, and so on. Allegedly retired American officers were sent to serve as instructors in Bosnia-Herzegovina for the Muslim-Croat army, just as they had done earlier in Croatia.

Combat operations developed, advancing from north to south and finally moving into the territory of Serbia, that is into Kosovo. The blucprint, on the basis of which the destruction of Yugoslavia and war against Yugoslavia had been planned, Kosovo being the last phase, was very simple. Paramilitary rebel forces, criminal groups and terrorists, and in Kosovo the narco Mafia were relied upon. During this time, the legitimate armed forces (the JNA and later the army of Yugoslavia) stood accused.

Tens of thousands of bombs and diverse projectile weapons, all with depleted uranium and still unidentified toxins, were dropped in open aggression on the remainder of Yugoslavia, that is, Serbia and Montenegro. As world experts have determined, five to six times more toxic material was dropped over Yugoslavia in the 1999 NATO aggression than had been dropped on Hiroshima. The involvement of the West, above all of Germany and the Vatican, was evident from the very beginning. Donald Horowitz presented arguments confirming that ethnic and national conflicts turn into the most brutal form of warfare when one or both sides gain international support. And this is precisely what happened on the territory of Yugoslavia.

The war on this territory was a synchronized action by secessionist and foreign forces that were planted in Yugoslav soil in large numbers and prepared to fuel the bloodshed. These are the Ustasha extremists, the Nazis, Islamic fundamentalists and Albanian terrorists whose role in the prevailing tensions was to serve as detonators for the outbreak of the conflict. The external forces in the initial phases acted behind the scenes, supplying the secessionists with arms and money, and infiltrating mercenaries into the country.

The final destruction of Yugoslavia was perpetrated through institutional deceptions. In the Helsinki Final Act, the European countries and the United States committed themselves to respect the territorial integrity of all signatory countries. Accordingly, they would refrain from any action directed against the territorial integrity, political independence and unity of every signatory country. This is article 4.

These principles were solemnly confirmed in Paris in 1990 with the signing of the Paris Charter. Only one year later, the European Community came out openly on the political scene as the striking force for the destruction of Yugoslavia.

In Brioni on July 7, 1991, a declaration was signed for the peaceful resolution of the conflict between the federal units of the SFRY.[4]

The European Community, relying on these aforementioned documents, was committed to seek a peaceful and lasting solution for the crisis between the federal units in Yugoslavia that would respect the territorial integrity of the country, from which, as the sole legally recognized entity, it received a mandate to mediate the conflict. The history of the civilized world demonstrates that the mediation process starts with a diagnosis of the causes of conflict, then proposes several possible solutions, leading to concessions that would be acceptable. Instead of all this, Lord Carrington,[5] at an extraordinary meeting of the Conference on Yugoslavia on October 18, 1991, presented, with no alternative, an ultimatum for the disappearance of Yugoslavia as a state and subject of international law. [The implementation of] such an ultimatum would reshape the territory of Yugoslavia on the model adopted by Hitler in 1941. Nazi values won the day. The right to the destruction of a state and secession was given priority over the right to preserve a state, the right to preserve a member state of the United Nations.

The paradox is that these same states deny the right to rebellion on their own territory — the English to the Irish, the Spaniards to the Basques, the French to the Corsicans, and so on. One should recall that when Serbian fighters fought together with the allies in World War II, the troops of the so-called Independent State of Croatia, as well as some from Bosnia, then within the NDH,[6] fought on the side of the Nazi forces. At that time, the infamous Handzar Division was sent to France as part of the convicts unit, and there they committed well-known grievous crimes.

Let us return to the Carrington document, which delivered the first blow against the sovereignty of Yugoslavia. Carrington's paper is an evident deception. With it, further negotiations were transformed into a farce. What followed was the recognition of the secessionist republics under strong pressure from Germany and the Vatican, contrary to the elementary principles of international law, the practice of the United Nations, and the practice of the leading power, the United States. Namely, under the Smithson declaration of January 7, 1932, the United States was committed to deny recognition to countries arising from violent upheavals. This principle first emerged as a regional rule of the American states, and then entered the universal rules of international law. America, yet once again, trampled its own law. In July 1991, that is, before the war started, Germany's Minister of Foreign Affairs, [Hans-Dietrich] Genscher, advocated immediate recognition of Slovenia and Croatia. And the Vatican was waging a parallel action. According to the United States Ambassador to the Holy See, Thomas Patrick Milady, as early as mid-1991, the Vatican initiated an action unprecedented in history by taking the leading role in lobbying for the recognition of these secessionist republics. The Vatican was exerting relentless pressure on European countries to recognize Croatia and Slovenia. In August 1991, Pope John Paul II dispatched Archbishop Torano to Yugoslavia. On his return, the Archbishop submitted a report stating that Serbia was indisputably the aggressor.

Yet another replacement of a thesis, yet another shameless lie and act of hypocrisy, and this time from a spiritual leader. Aggression against one's own country is something that can only be conceived with extremely malicious intent. The press, however, accepted this view. According to Milady, there was perfect coordination between the Vatican and Germany. In mid-December 1991, Genscher visited the Vatican. On his return on December 19, he announced that Germany would recognize Croatia and Slovenia, regardless of the position of other countries. And this was carried out on December 23. The Vatican did this on January 13, 1992.

Germany and the Vatican were led in this matter by their historic geostrategic interests. They had worked on the destruction of Yugoslavia for years. This was unequivocally stated in the prestigious magazine *Politics International*, issue 66, 1994-95, by Helmut Kohl, who emphasized that the history of contemporary Yugoslavia constitutes an unbreakable unity with the history of the old Yugoslavia.

The decisive period started when [Klaus] Kinkel became head of security services in Germany and established very close links with Ustasha émigrés. According to the well-known American analyst Eric Schmidt Burnham,[7] the key figures inside the country who were working on the destruction of Yugoslavia were Josip Malovic, Josip Bojkovac, Franjo Tudjman, and the then Croatian President Stjepan Mesic.

Mesic confirmed his role on Slovenian television when he stated that the idea of the break-up, I quote, "of Yugoslavia was something [I] wanted to transmit to those who had the strongest influence on its fate, Genscher and the Pope." And he continued, "I met Genscher three times. He facilitated my contact with the Holy See. The Pope and Genscher agreed on the total break-up of Yugoslavia." Then came the recognition of Croatia and Slovenia, followed by other countries of the European Community in January 1992. In the case of Bosnia-Herzegovina, this occurred on April 6 of the same year, the very date of Hitler's attack on Yugoslavia in 1941.

As stated in each individual act of recognition, the federal entities were recognized with internationally recognized borders; however the administrative borders had never been recognized as international by any international document. There is not even one single internal act with regard to these borders, nor did one ever exist. What is most important in all this is that such recognition was a one-sided political act, whereas the problem of establishing borders is a complex, multi-level legal process. Therefore, fictitious — not real — state borders were recognized.

The units that were recognized did not meet the elementary preconditions for statehood. It is undisputed in scholarly literature that a state needs to have a legitimate state apparatus, stable political and legal structures, a monopoly of power within the territory, and full control over the use of that power in order to be recognized as a state. And, most importantly, the state must demonstrate the strength and readiness to fulfill international responsibilities and to provide internal security.

None of these requirements had been met at the time of the recognition, which was granted during a bloody civil war, and this will be recorded as an event unique in modern history, but in a very negative sense.

Erroneous Recognition

The recognition of rebel forces caused great astonishment and was condemned in legal circles, as it was elsewhere, throughout the world. Cedric Thornberry, the leader of the civil sector of the UNPROFOR, states in his memoirs,[8] and I quote: "When Ambassador Cutileiro[9] notified us of the decision of recognition, General Morillon[10] and I were astonished." The widely circulated French newspaper *Figaro* called this "an exercise in legal hypocrisy." General MacKenzie[11] states in his memoirs:[12] "Although we were not diplomats, all of us in uniform were sure that fighting would break out all around us as soon as recognition was announced." Special envoy to the UN, Cyrus Vance,[13] stated that recognition of Slovenia, Croatia, and Bosnia and Herzegovina by the European Community and the USA, I quote: "Led to the war that is being waged on the territory of Yugoslavia." He made this statement in September 1992.

The recognition of fictitious states in a civil war represents an indirect form of aggression against the Socialist Federal Republic of Yugoslavia.

The secessionist republics, aided by a powerful media campaign and the deceit of the international community, were accepted as members of the United Nations in flagrant violation of international law and the UN Charter. Sanctions were imposed on the rest of Yugoslavia, the original core of Yugoslavia, in May 1992, and the country was isolated. In July of the same year, Yugoslavia's membership in the United Nations was suspended only because we did not accept the deletion, by the stroke of a pen, of the existing state in which we had lived.

Such legal chaos, such moral decline of the leading powers in the post-Cold War period, and of the Vatican, opened the way to madness and lawlessness from the borders in the north to Kosovo and the extreme south. This *ad hoc* Tribunal was also established with the sole objective of covering up the heaping pile of mistakes made by Western policy and justifying its crimes — the destruction of a state and the high technology barbarism committed by NATO countries in their three-month-long bombardment of Yugoslavia, the mass crimes against its citizens, and the destruction of the medieval heritage of the Serbian people in Kosovo, and so on.

A very transparent tactic was used, whose purpose was to close the circle and to render logical thinking based on empirical data impossible by instrumentalizing extremely complex events on the territory of Yugoslavia and by placing the responsibility on Serbia as the aggressor, and on me personally.

Senseless, even vulgar theories of bad guys and rogue states cannot overshadow historical facts and the historical responsibility for the tragedy of one European state. A joint criminal intent did exist, but it did not proceed from Belgrade, nor did it exist in Belgrade. Quite to the contrary, it existed among the joint forces of the secessionists, Germany and the Vatican, as well as other countries in the European Union and the USA.

The Illegitimacy of the Tribunal

I questioned the legality of this so-called Tribunal during my first appearance here and then on a number of occasions since then. You have provided me with an abundance of arguments in support of my position during the trial. I will not dwell on the absence of a legal basis for the establishment of this Tribunal. I would just like to remind you that the source of judicial power can only come from international treaties, and not from resolutions, as stated by the UN Secretary-General himself in a statement to the Security Council on May 3, 1993. Therefore, you owe the international community an answer: Where does the UN Security Council derive the power to suspend implementation of international treaties? I have in mind the Geneva Conventions of 1949, the Additional Protocols, and the Convention for the Prevention and Punishment of Genocide of 1948, all of which place the responsibility for trials of war crimes in national courts. An international court may have authority only if it were created by a *lege artis* and only if it is of general nature. This so-called Tribunal lacks both elements. The act of establishing this Tribunal is individual in nature and it is, therefore, a political act.

The elementary legal principle is equality before the law. This raises the question: why have courts not been formed for all the wars that are being waged throughout the world or, at least, which have been waged in the last decade of the twentieth century? Although there are no principled reasons for not doing something like that, if such a thing were legal, it should apply to all.

In other words, this Tribunal represents the most serious form of discrimination against one country and it is a grievous trampling of the Convention prohibiting all forms of discrimination. At the very beginning, I requested that this institution use its authority under Article 96 of the UN Charter to seek permission from the General Assembly to ask the International Court of Justice — this legal and highest institutional level of jurisdiction in the UN system, which is authorized to interpret the Charter — to provide a legal opinion on whether the resolutions of the Security Council establishing this Tribunal were in accordance with the UN Charter or not.

The fact that this Tribunal has given itself the right to decide whether it was established in a legally valid manner and then concluded, as could be expected, that it was legally constituted, does not at all mean that this conclusion is correct, or that the Tribunal even had the authority to draw such a conclusion. Namely, this so-called court, just like any other court, is absolutely not authorized to render judgment on its own legality. That is why its decision on this issue is legally invalid. Courts are authorized to decide on their own authority: whether they are competent or not; whether they are competent to decide a question or not. However, the question of the jurisdiction of a court and the question of its legality are two separate issues. The question of legality has precedence over the question of authority, because if a court is not legal, then the question of its jurisdiction is pointless.

As opposed to the question of its own authority, no court, nor any other organ, has the authority to decide the matter of its own legality, because law, by tradition, forbids one to render a judgment in one's own case (*judi inclusa sua*). But, on the other hand, this illegal Tribunal does not have the right to deprive persons standing before it of an answer with respect to whether or not they are facing a legal or an illegal organ, particularly if there is a legally valid manner, which I have pointed out, to resolve such a question, and by refusing to resort to this, the person in question facing this court is then denied justice (*deni de justice*).

I am afraid, however, that the people who have authority in this institution are aware that the International Court of Justice would rule in accordance with the views of the previous President of the International Court of Justice Mohammed Bedjaoui, who in his book *The New World Order and the Security Council: Testing the Legality of Its Acts*, cites both Resolutions relating to this Tribunal to be among the acts or laws that he considers controversial.

Therefore, this Tribunal is not an International Tribunal, and much less an independent organ, as you wish to present it. An ideological fiction has been created for public consumption: "The International Community," which is allegedly behind this Tribunal, is actually a gross deception. The idea to establish the Tribunal came from Kinkel after he succeeded Genscher, the principal war criminal in the destruction of Yugoslavia. The idea was taken over by Madeleine Albright,[14] and the costs of the preliminary activities, as well as later activities, were funded by the Soros Foundation. Soros also founded the Coalition for International Justice, an NGO, in order to provide "assistance" to the Tribunal.

Members of this and other so-called NGOs, some of whom are employed by this Tribunal today, were engaged in 1992 in Bosnia-Herzegovina to gather evidence of alleged Serbian crimes.

Albright presented this before the U.S. Congress, and engaged different lobbies and different media for the purpose of fabricating a certain image that would influence public opinion. She was called "the mother of the Tribunal" in the U.S. Congress. As for the authenticity of the evidence given by the NGOs, we can use the scandal in connection with the false documents presented by the representatives of those organizations as the basis for the charges against me for alleged crimes in Kosovo. The journalist from *The New York Times*[15] who wrote an article based on this false information was forced to resign for professional and ethical reasons.

I even have that issue of *The New York Times* here, but I don't have the time to present it. The drafter of the Statutes of the Tribunal, Michael Scharf, gave a very precise assessment of the Tribunal in an interview to the *Washington Post* on October 3, 1999, and he pointed out, and I quote: "The tribunal was ... a potentially useful policy tool ... to isolate offending leaders diplomatically, ... and fortify the international political will to employ sanctions or use force."

In other words, the Tribunal is an instrument of war — not of peace. This was confirmed in the respectable Canadian newspaper, *The Globe and Mail* by Marcus McGee, who stressed that the Tribunal, and I quote: "is part of NATO's war strategy." So this is some kind of private justice known only to those who had a coalition war imposed on them and the intention is to revert to a jurisprudence of the early middle ages.

Eminent attorneys around the world refer to this Tribunal as NATO's propaganda weapon. So there can be no question of any independence at all. We also need to add the fact that since 1996 the NATO Secretary-General has been in constant communication with your Chief Prosecutor. On May 9, 1996, a memorandum was signed by the Chief Prosecutor and the Supreme Commander of NATO for Europe about the modalities of operation. Therefore, NATO — and not the United Nations — has taken the role of the Tribunal policeman, and that is why this Tribunal cannot be considered as an international institution at all, but a NATO institution. There is another factor supporting this claim. Your own article 32 of the Statutes provides that expenses for the Tribunal should be covered by the regular budget of the United Nations, but in practice the money comes from very questionable sources like, for example, the Soros Foundation and foundations of various Islamic countries. The bulk of the money comes from NATO itself. According to NATO spokesman Jamie Shea, and I quote: "NATO countries are in the forefront of those who ... fund these Tribunals." He stated this on May 17, 1999, in Pristina. We also need to recall that Soros funding goes to the so-called "Kosovo Liberation Army," which is, in fact, the KLA terrorist organization, and its main propaganda newspaper, *Koha Ditore*.

Germany's Role

Genscher stated during the signing of the treaty regarding the final status of Germany on September 12, 1990, in Moscow, with the foreign ministers of the Democratic Republic of Germany, France, Great Britain, the Soviet Union, and the United States that: "We do not want anything else other than to live with all other nations in freedom, democracy and peace. State unity represents for us greater responsibility but not aspirations for greater power."

Chancellor Kohl, on October 3, the day commemorating Germany's reunification, sent a message to all world governments, including the Yugoslav government, in which, amongst other things, he said: "In the future only peace will emanate from German territory. We are aware that the inviolability of borders and the respect for the territorial integrity of all states in Europe form the basic conditions for peace. In addition, we have moral and legal obligations which arise from German history."

These are big words and big promises that were given to the rest of humanity — and in particular Europe — at the moment when the

German nation finally was allowed to cast off the burden of its division, which was imposed on it precisely because of the darkest period of German history.

Yes, those were big words and promises, but at the same time they were empty words and empty promises. For how the top German leadership views the moral and legal obligations arising from German history, which they cite, and what their relation is to the inviolability of borders and respect for territorial integrity and sovereignty of all states in Europe as the basic condition for peace could be clearly seen in practice at the same time in the case of Yugoslavia. German twentieth-century history had inflicted a cost of three million lives in the territory of this state: a death toll of 1,247,000 Serbs in the First World War, and 1,700,000 Yugoslavs dead in World War II.

It was precisely in October 1990, the month of German reunification, that the security services of the Yugoslav People's Army uncovered and managed to secretly tape activities pertaining to the illegal importation of weapons to Croatia with the aim of facilitating the armed secession of Croatia. This was the actual break-up of the territorial integrity of Yugoslavia. The illegal importation of weapons went through Hungary, but the largest part of weapons came from the already reunited Germany, which made Chancellor Kohl's cited promise, that only peace would emanate from German territory, an irony.

Arming secessionists was not the sole or the first type of German involvement in the internal affairs of Yugoslavia; it contributed to deepening — if not to originating — the Yugoslav crisis. All of the activities of Slovenia and Croatia in the violent achievement of independence were not only supported and aided by Germany, but to a considerable degree they were encouraged by its top state leaders. The Presidency of Yugoslavia and the leaders of the Yugoslav republics gathered in Belgrade on August 20 and 21, 1991, in an effort to put an end to the conflict in the territory of Croatia as well as to stop the attacks on the JNA. They adopted several decisions for the purpose of stabilizing the situation. A minimum program of political and economic cooperation was adopted, a commission was formed to develop agreements on the future form of the multinational state, and an agreement was also reached to conduct a meeting between the leadership of the JNA and the Republic of Croatia. On August 20, there was an extraordinary ministerial session on European political cooperation in which the ministers of foreign affairs of the member states of the European Union concluded that they welcomed the readiness of all parties to embark on negotiations about the future of Yugoslavia, and they requested all sides to conduct negotiations in goodwill among themselves. But, on that very same day, Genscher held a consultative meeting with the foreign ministers of Slovenia and Croatia. On August 24, 1991, he met with Boris Frlec, a Slovene, who was the Yugoslav ambassador in Bonn, which guaranteed that the message directed to the Yugoslav authorities would also be passed on to Ljubljana and Zagreb, and he told him: "If the bloodshed continues, and if the policy of violence supported by the JNA is not stopped immediately, the federal government will have to seriously consider the recognition of Slovenia and Croatia within their existing borders. It will also conduct a review of these matters within the European Community."

The question arises: Was better and greater impetus and encouragement needed for those who had already proclaimed secession and who had already resorted to the use of weapons in order to achieve it, or was more encouragement needed to maintain the cease-fire? The message that came was that continued bloodshed would lead to the recognition of these states, and unfortunately that is what happened.

The message produced the desired effect because Croatian paramilitary forces broke the cease-fire that had already been agreed upon and proceeded to escalate the conflict. Finally, Lord [David] Owen,[16] whose book[17] you have included here, also speaks about Germany's readiness to support Slovenia and Croatia in their illegal secession through recognition, even at the cost of serious clashes with its partners from the European Community and the United States. He, I remind you, says that Genscher's letter to Perez de Cuellar,[18] written in German, referred to public statements exacerbating tensions in Yugoslavia and to the Treaty of Paris but, as Perez de Cuellar reminded him in his reply, Genscher omitted to mention the EC Declaration issued in Rome on November 8, 1991, which stated that the prospect of recognition of the independence of those Republics wishing it, can only be envisaged in the framework of an overall settlement.

Therefore, as Owen reminds us, in addition to the Declaration of the European Community of March 26, 1991, which supported the unity of Yugoslavia, the European Community on November 8, 1991, adopted a Declaration calling for the attainment of "a comprehensive solution." Nevertheless, the German position finally did prevail, and once the Pandora's box was opened and once the illegal secession was recognized at the cost of human lives, it was difficult to stop the bloodletting process since matters had not been stopped in Croatia and Slovenia, again regardless of consequences. A further step was taken.

At the end of the first paragraph, on page 344 of his book, Lord Owen says that "the European Community's mistake over recognizing Croatia could have been overcome if it had not been compounded by going forward regardless of the consequences with the recognition of Bosnia and Herzegovina. The U.S., which had opposed the recognition of Croatia in December 1991, became very active in pushing for recognition of Bosnia and Herzegovina in the spring of 1992. Yet it should not have been judged inevitable, nor indeed was it logical, to push ahead and recognize Bosnia and Herzegovina, an internal republic of Yugoslavia that contained three large constituent peoples with very different views on independence."

So one mistake followed the other, one impudence followed another, and the cost was paid in human lives. And when human lives are the price that has to be paid, then such mistakes and impudence turn into crime. In this case, it was crime against peace, precisely the kind of crime for which this illegal institution does not have jurisdiction, none whatsoever. The U.S. Secretary of State, Warren Christopher, in his interview in the newspaper *USA Today*, which was also carried by *Die Welt* on June 18, 1993, confirmed that Germany was the crucial culprit for the escalation of the Yugoslav crisis. Christopher said that during the overall process of recognition, and especially the premature recognition, grave mistakes were made for which Germany bears special responsibility. Many experts are of the opinion that the problems we confront today stem from the recognition of Croatia and Bosnia.

Christopher's French colleague Roland Dumas, in a statement reported in the *Deutsche Zeitung* of June 21, 1993, criticized the European Community for recognizing Slovenia and Croatia, I quote, "in a hasty and precipitous manner, which paved the way for the break-up of Yugoslavia," and said, I quote: "The responsibility of Germany and the Vatican for the escalation of the crisis is obviously enormous."

Another direct participant in these events, the Dutch Prime Minister at the time, Rudd Lubbers, said in 1997 that German Chancellor Kohl exerted pressure on the European Community to change its position that the independence of Croatia should not be recognized in order to avoid further escalation of the civil war. In connection with this, he said, and I quote: "The Minister of Foreign Affairs, [Hans] Van den Broek and I could have stood on our heads, the other Europeans could only look around in astonishment, and the Germans eagerly did the job by themselves. That was a catastrophe." The quote is from *Au Courant* of December 21, 1997. When all that has been written about German support for Croatian and Slovenian secessionists in their efforts to carry out their plan is considered, then those statements made by Stjepan Mesic about the role of Genscher and Pope John Paul II on the televised "Contact Program" should come as no surprise. But if Germany's aggressive support for the break-up of Yugoslavia and the recognition of the secession of its break-away republics is self-evident and widely known to the public by now, for many the question remains: What are the motives for such actions and such obstinate persistence on the part of the top leadership of recently reunited Germany? This question is answered by General Pierre-Marie Gallois, one of the world's leading experts on geopolitics and a close associate of de Gaulle. In an interview for *Die Zeit* on July 23, 1993, he said the following: "The break-up of this country and the linking of Croats and Slovenes to German industry led to the emancipation of these peoples who once were associated with the Empire in the heart of Europe and then with the Third Reich. On the other hand, that meant punishment of the Serbs, who, in both world wars, persistently stood by the allies. Thirdly, this led to the disappearance of the last remnants of those treaties that punished Germany twice for its defeats."

Although many would look with suspicion and disapproval upon these views of the old French general and eminent anti-fascist, believing that Germany's historic ambitions are just a matter of the distant past and that the new historical circumstances as well as the catharsis that the German nation went through are sufficient guarantees to believe in the peace-loving assurances of German politicians given during the events occasioned by the reunification of Germany, it is sufficient to be reminded of Klaus Kinkel's article entitled "German Foreign Policy in Light of the New Order," published in the *Frankfurter Allgemeine Zeitung* on March 19, 1993. In this article, the task of German foreign policy is expressed as follows: "To achieve something in relation to the outside world where in the past we have failed twice." It is quite clear what this means. There is probably no one in the world who does not understand where it was that Germany failed twice in the outside world. Therefore, according to the foreign minister of Germany himself, the task of the foreign policy of this country is to use its potential to achieve what it did not achieve through two world wars, and the question that remains is whether this will be resolved through old or new means.

Kohl himself, in connection with the recognition of Croatia's secession, said in a television program: "There is an especially close relationship between Germans and Croats that has a great deal to do with history." This historical vertical that Kohl pointed to in German foreign policy explains the actions that Kinkel pointed to as well. Finally, there is also a similar vertical in the actions and policy of their Croatian cronies, which sometimes strikingly reflect actions and words almost identical to the actors during the two world wars and the war against Yugoslavia during the nineties of the twentieth century. Thus, during three wars the constant element of the German policy in the Balkans has been anti-Yugoslav pressure. First, there were bloody efforts in order to prevent the creation of the Yugoslav state, and later on even more bloodshed to break up the country and wipe it from the face of the earth.

The Myth of "Greater Serbia"

The key thread that extends through the rhetoric and policy of the German block, that is Austria, or rather Austria-Hungary and Germany, in the Balkans is the theory of the danger of the creation of a Greater Serbia. This danger, this key thesis has taken a central place in this false indictment against me. A Greater Serbia is the thesis and myth that was created by Austro-Hungarian propaganda as far back as the second half of the nineteenth century. It is an integral part of the efforts made by a "rotting empire" to keep its occupied Southern Slav territories. This was the fear that the South Slav peoples under Austro-Hungarian occupation — carried by the wave of a broad European movement for national emancipation and liberation from occupation by a number of European nations, and for unification of divided territories into one state as was the case with Germany — might achieve unification, although there was a natural and historical legitimacy involved with respect to the unification of the Southern Slavs.

Another German, Ambassador Ralf Hartman, in his book *The Honorable Mediators*, on page 31 says as follows: "This illustrates the depth of this fear and how far back it goes into the past. Already in 1876, when the Serbian Prince Milan gave his support to the rebellion of the Christian population of Herzegovina and Bosnia against Turkish rule and declared war on Istanbul, [Russia's Chancellor] Prince Gorchakov, German Chancellor Bismarck and the Austro-Hungarian Prime Minister Andrassy, under Habsburg pressure, agreed in the so-called Berlin memorandum that in case the Serbs won," and he quotes "the powers will not tolerate the creation of a large Slav state."

So what was an understandably natural right for all others — Germans, Russians, English, French, Spaniards and Italians — in the 19th century to live in a single state, was to be denied to the South Slavs, that is to the Serbs, forever. Their aspirations for national unification were called a heresy and presented as a threatening specter. The name of that specter was Serbia. Although the Serbian Kingdom, in spite of all its aspirations, was small and weak compared to the great European powers (the Serbian population never exceeded ten million), this specter remained in Vienna, in Berlin and elsewhere for decades, and continues to live until the present day. This indictment is the best proof of how true what I am saying is, because these specters are involved here.

What is particularly striking is the fact that starting with Austro-Hungarian propaganda, liberation from the centuries-old yoke of Ottoman and Habsburg rule, and the unification of the South Slavs — not only the Serbs — was treated and referred to as an aspiration for the creation of Greater Serbia, that is, the expansion of the Serbian state. And this formulation implies the existence of some kind of expansionist tendencies, tendencies among Serbs for conquest. This, contrary to the fact that the formulation of the idea of the South Slavs — not only the Serbs but all South Slavs — grew among the South Slav peoples under foreign rule, who planted the roots that would lead to the creation of the Yugoslav idea.

The root of the Yugoslav idea was born among the Croatian people. In spite of this, when the Serbs espoused this in order to help their enslaved brothers in Austria-Hungary, that idea remained as an idea of Greater Serbia — equating two concepts that are absolutely not the same, between Yugoslavia, the joint state of the South Slav peoples, and some kind of Greater Serbia, as a product and weapon of anti-Yugoslav and anti-Serb propaganda. So then and now, behind all this is the aspiration to dominate and control the territories populated by South Slavs and to keep these peoples enslaved, while hiding under the propaganda smokescreen that it is

Serbia that has such intentions, and that Serbia is attempting to expand into territories that belong to others. And this is a sheer lie.

I have another quotation from the German archives, showing how the German ambassador conveyed to his government the content of his discussions with Count Berchtold, the Foreign Minister of Austria-Hungary. The Minister said, and I quote from the archives of the ministry in Vienna, that he considered it "his obligation not to leave the German government uninformed about the seriousness of the position of the monarchy." According to him, "the South Slav question, that is to say the unhindered possession of the provinces inhabited by the South Slavs, is a question of life and death for the monarchy, as well as the Triple Alliance.[19] The South Slav provinces of the monarchy could not be held in the face of Serbia's supremacy in the Balkans. Accordingly, the monarchy may be forced to intervene if Serbia defeats Bulgaria and annexes territories beyond the boundaries of Old Serbia. To my question, what he thinks about when and how such action would take place, the minister noted that a good psychological moment could be found." A pretext came soon, the well-known Sarajevo assassination, when Gavrilo Princip, a member of the organization Young Bosnia, assassinated [Archduke Franz] Ferdinand, heir to the Austro-Hungarian throne. Nothing has ever been said about the fact that twenty young men of Serbian, Croatian and Muslim nationality took part in that assassination conspiracy. This was Young Bosnia. And it has never been established if there were any involvement at all in that assassination on the part of the Kingdom of Serbia. Nevertheless, accusations were immediately leveled against Serbia and the Serbian people, while Austria-Hungary and Germany were gripped by a veritable anti-Serbian hysteria. In his aforementioned book, Ambassador Hartman says: "In Austria-Hungary and Germany a fierce anti-Serbian campaign was launched, overshadowing everything else, inspiring the German Ambassador in London, Lichnovski, to remind the German Secretary of State in the Ministry of Foreign Affairs, Gottlieb von Jagow, that the entire Serbian nation had to be stigmatized as a race of evil-doers and assassins."

This is obviously something that challenges the basic premise of this indictment and its approach. Even more so since this has lasted for so many decades. The truth is that no one wanted to seriously consider and fundamentally examine the essence and the meaning of this evil above all evils, Greater Serbia. Hence, here too, it has been used in a very facile and arrogant manner. Nobody is investigating the essence and meaning, the genesis and development of such "evil," for had it been done, all this propaganda would have burst like a soap bubble. It is well known that on June 23, 1914, the Serbian government was presented with an ultimatum by Austria-Hungary, based on false accusations of Serbia's involvement in this assassination, imposing a number of demands upon Serbia, which no country in the world could have accepted.

Any normal person has to be astonished by the text of this ultimatum, whose rejection was expected and whose only purpose was to specifically act as a pretext for war. Just like what happened in Rambouillet. The British Minister of Foreign Affairs, Sir Edward Grey, was also astonished. He characterized this document as, and I quote, "the most formidable demand ... ever imposed on one state by another."

Grey would never have suspected that the Serbian people and the Serbian state would be exposed to a number of similar, perhaps even more impudent and even more astounding ultimatums in that same century; that his state Great Britain, with Germany, Austria, and some other Western countries, even some Serbian allies from that time, especially France and somewhat later the USA, would co-author and issue new ultimatums, just as it would co-author and participate in the implementation of murderous assaults on the Serbian people at the end of the twentieth century, carried out by means of unscrupulous lies and merciless economic sanctions, and finally, also participate in bestial military attacks against its former Serbian allies whose crowning sin was that they tried to protect their country and their people and preserve what they had acquired through great sacrifices with the help of allies in two world wars.

It is hard to imagine the shame Sir Edward Grey would have felt had he known what an important role his country would play in completing this decades-long crime against the Serbian people at the end of the twentieth century, which is being carried out here, before this institution, in flagrant violation of international law and elementary human morals. For perhaps it is precisely the resolution that established this illegal Tribunal that Sir Edward Grey would have defined as "the most astounding document ever engineered by diplomacy."

It is well known how the Kingdom of the Serbs, Croats and Slovenes (later renamed Yugoslavia) was established as the common state of the South Slav peoples, whose creation the German block sought ardently to prevent. It failed to make this state vanish from the face of the earth in World War I and later in World War II. However, the old myth of Greater Serbia remained as a proven smokescreen for concealing their own crimes behind someone else's fabricated sin. It is in this institution that the lie of Greater Serbia found its natural foundation and grew into a monstrous construction of foreboding magnitude, to make the irony and absurdity even greater and to make the lies and injustice against the Serbian people all the more horrible and perfidious.

In contrast to their Balkan neighbors, it is only the Serbian people in this region, although they had ample opportunity and much greater opportunity than others, who did not attempt to create their own extended state. It is well known that in 1915, the allies of Serbia, in the so-called London Treaty, offered Serbia, after winning the war, an extension of its territory to Bosnia and Herzegovina, parts of Dalmatia, parts of Slavonia, and so forth. There are documents that show all this. But Serbia did not do this. Serbia instead embraced and espoused Serbs, Croats and Slovenes alike from the former territories of the Austro-Hungarian Empire, and this is how the Kingdom of Serbs, Croats and Slovenes was created, later to be called Yugoslavia.

This option was taken by the Serbian state, to create the common state of Yugoslavia — and not the Serbian state — that extended protection to our Croatian and Slovenian brothers from territorial fragmentation and from being part of a defeated state, to joining the winning camp. In spite of this, however, the Serbs were branded with the stamp of Greater Serbia precisely in those last throes of the disintegrating Habsburg monarchy, and this historic lie has been sustained to this very day.

In order to understand the whole matter, it is useful to look at the situation from the other side of the front in World War I. Namely, in 1915, the German theoretician Friedrich Naumann published his book *Central Europe* (*Mitteleuropa*), in which he presented a project for the reorganization of Europe. Of course, it was then expected that the Germans would win the war and the reorganization of Europe would involve the creation of a greater Germany that would encompass all of Central Europe surrounded by small, weak states, which Naumann called "Trabant[20] states" in his book. They would be....

JUDGE PATRICK ROBINSON: Mr. Milosevic, you have to be shorter in the second part of your statement.

PRESIDENT SLOBODAN MILOSEVIC: Mr. Robinson, I understand that it is already 10:30. But, I hope you are aware of the fact that the interpreters often tell me to slow down. Therefore, I think that it would be appropriate if you would consider extending my time beyond today and give me some time tomorrow, as well. It is obvious....

JUDGE PATRICK ROBINSON: Mr. Milosevic, I am against that and I suggest that you provide the written copy of your speech.

PRESIDENT SLOBODAN MILOSEVIC: Mr. Robinson, I do not have anything in writing. I just have my notes. So I cannot give them my notes. They would not be able to read my handwriting anyway. The typed material for preparations that I do have would be completely useless to them. That's why I asked you to consider...

JUDGE PATRICK ROBINSON: Very well, Mr. Milosevic. Very well. We will adjourn for half an hour.

Recess taken at 10:31 a.m.

On resuming at 11:05 a.m.

JUDGE PATRICK ROBINSON: Mr. Milosevic, you may continue.

PRESIDENT SLOBODAN MILOSEVIC: Isn't the microphone working? Is it working now? Yes. It's all right now. All right. Thank you.

I mentioned Friedrich Naumann, the German theoretician, who, in his book *Central Europe* described a greater Germany surrounded by satellite states which would be completely dependent on the great and powerful German state. Naumann does not mention Serbia as a satellite state because, according to him, Serbia is, "like a fortress that is in the way in this area and has to be wiped off the map."

Let me mention that this creator of the greater German project, which implies the elimination of Serbia from the map of Europe, in accordance with the anti-Serbian propaganda waged at that time and the well-known slogan of the time, "Serbia must die" ("Serbien muss sterben"), is considered to be the ideologue of the Liberal Party in Germany, a party which has long served to balance the German political scene and which was in charge of German foreign policy for more that two decades. This is the era of Genscher and Kinkel, that same Kinkel who in 1993 felt the need to proclaim

[and] publicize the idea of revisionism, which had already started, of Germany's past historical course and results: "Something has to be done externally that we have twice failed to do."

The Destruction of Yugoslavia

The importance attached by German Liberals, especially by the two above-mentioned leaders of German diplomacy, to the ideas of Friedrich Naumann is best seen in the fact that the foundation established by the Liberal Party is named the Friedrich Naumann Foundation. The loyal and strict adherence to the substance of his plan is best reflected in the frenzied and destructive efforts made by Genscher and Kinkel against Yugoslavia and Serbia, and in aspiring to affirm and confirm German domination of Europe through the fragmentation of Central European and East European space. And this, in fact, did take place. You have the example of Czechoslovakia, not to mention the destruction of the USSR, the leading victorious power in the Second World War.

When Serbia was sentenced to death by this distorted approach of the exponents of greater German hegemonic aspirations and had submerged its statehood in the newly created state of South Slavs, thereby negating most eloquently the propaganda lies about tendencies and aspirations for a Greater Serbia, it was only natural for the death sentence to be transferred to the newly established state of Yugoslavia. It is well known that in Serbia in 1941, when the government decided to forge an alliance with Hitler and the Tripartite Pact,[21] large-scale demonstrations protested this act, and overthrew the government. Churchill then said, "Yugoslavia has found its soul again." This was stated on one side, the side of the allies. On the other side, Hitler stated on the day Yugoslavia was attacked that this military attack was directed against, and I quote, "the same criminal clique, those same creatures who, through the assassination in Sarajevo, pushed the world into unspeakable misfortune." How much does this assertion remind us of the assertion made by a new Fuehrer fifty-eight years later, on the eve of a new bombardment of Serbia and Yugoslavia. Namely Clinton, president of the USA at the time, on the night of March 24, while explaining to the American public via television the decision to launch, as he called it, an air campaign against Yugoslavia, pointed out that the Serbs not only caused World War I, but that without them, there would have been no "holocaust." So much for the knowledge of and respect for history of these two criminals.

The rest is contained in the German archives, in memoranda from Hitler's meetings: the Fuehrer was determined to destroy Yugoslavia both militarily and as a state. The destruction of Yugoslavia, as a creation of statecraft, can easily be linked to the "mission accomplished" message given by the President of the Presidency of Yugoslavia up until that time, Stjepan Mesic, in a well-known report, celebrated for its evil and cynicism, to the Croatian Parliament on December 5, 1991. And I quote: "Thank you for the confidence you have placed in me to fight for the interests of Croatia in the segment entrusted to me. I think I have accomplished the task. Yugoslavia does not exist anymore."

When speaking of these efforts and this crime, which was perpetrated against Yugoslavia as well as against other countries subject to such aggression, it is worth noting that directives were given in Germany for "questions of propaganda" before the attack on Yugoslavia. Ambassador Ralf Hartman speaks of well known traditional lines of German Balkan propaganda as follows: a) the enemy of Germany is exclusively the Serbian government, which fanned the flames of struggle against Germany; b) since the Serbs have implemented a ruthless dictatorship against the non-Serbian peoples in Yugoslavia, primarily the Croats and the Macedonians (which is completely absurd!), we must tell them clearly that the German *Wehrmacht* is not entering Yugoslavia as the enemy of Croats, Bosnians and Macedonians — moreover, that they will be protected from slaughter at the hands of Serbian chauvinists.

Protection from slaughter at the hands of "Serbian chauvinists" in the German puppet concoction, the Independent State of Croatia, resulted in a genocide conducted against the Serbs, Jews and Gypsies. One million Serbs were expelled from the territory of this monstrous state, and over half of them were driven to their death in circumstances of extreme and grievous suffering. Joseph Goebbels certainly contributed directives to this monstrous activity, which remained alive and relevant in later German political practice: cajole the Croats while stirring up their hatred of the Serbs.

It is more than obvious to what extent this German policy was applied in the Balkans at the end of the twentieth century. But this continuity in German policy is perhaps best illustrated in the following statement made by the Croatian leader Ante Pavelic in 1941: "I know that for the independence of Croatia, our gratitude is due solely to the might of the Fuehrer, the German Reich and Europe." That continuity is particularly obvious when this sentence is compared with the song *Danke Deutschland* [Thank You, Germany], sung in Croatia at the end of 1991 and the beginning of 1992, or to the assertions made by Stjepan Mesic about the especially important roles played by Genscher and Pope John Paul II in the break-up of Yugoslavia.

The Role of the Vatican

When we take the second key international actor into consideration — and, according to Mesic, the second key international actor in the break-up of Yugoslavia was the Holy See — it too is characterized by historical continuity in its anti-Yugoslav orientation and activity, as well as by the stability of its alliance with those who fought against the establishment of Yugoslavia before and during World War I, and with those who fought against Yugoslavia throughout its existence, in particular during World War II.

The following finding from a report by the Austro-Hungarian envoy to the Holy See sent to Vienna on July 27, 1914, that is, before war was declared against Serbia, attests to the deep roots of this Vatican policy as well as to the Vatican's war-mongering anti-Serbian propaganda, and I quote from his conversation with the secretary of state, Cardinal Mario del Vallo: "During the last year, His Holiness many times expressed his regret that Austria-Hungary failed to punish its dangerous Danubean neighbors. The Pope and the Curia see in Serbia a sickness that is slowly eating away at the essence of the monarchy whose extinction it will cause with time. For the Church, the destruction of this bastion would constitute the loss of its strongest defenders." The secretary of state, the Cardinal, expressed the hope that the monarchy would pursue this matter to the end.

Therefore, according to the official position of the Vatican, Serbia was to be destroyed in order to strengthen the Austro-Hungarian monarchy as the geopolitical stronghold of the Catholic Church in this area, and in particular to serve as its basis for expansion to the East. It is more than evident that this has nothing to do with the teachings of Christ, but it is also even more evident how much this has to do with the teachings two decades later by Adolf Hitler, who was obsessed with the crazed and bloody idea of his divine mission and his goal to advance the German "*Drang nach Osten.*" So it is not surprising that the Holy See headed by Pope Pius XII easily established an alliance with the Axis powers headed by Hitler. In Croatia, this alliance was achieved through the close ties of the Catholic Church with Pavelic's Independent State of Croatia, whose Minister of Education, Mile Budak, stated in Gospic: "One part of Serbs we will destroy, another part we will expel, the rest we will convert to the Catholic faith and turn into Croats. In this way, we will eradicate their traces and what will be left will be just a bad memory of them."

Professor Edmond Paris, in his book *Genocide in Satellite Croatia 1941-1945* (Chicago, 1961), says: "The greatest genocide during World War II, in proportion to a nation's population, took place not in Nazi Germany but in the puppet state of Croatia," which was created by the Nazis. Also, Professor Helen Fein, in her book *Accounting for Genocide* (New York, 1979), says, and I quote: "The state of Croatia ... instigated, planned and executed massacres against the Serbian Orthodox minority ... and that the Catholic clergy approved ... these massacres." According to McMillan's *Encyclopedia of the Holocaust*, pages 323 to 328, in the Independent State of Croatia, and I quote, "more than half a million Serbs were killed, a quarter million expelled, and two hundred thousand forced to convert to Catholicism."

The genocide conducted in the Independent State of Croatia against the Serbs is one of the most closely guarded secrets of the twentieth century, just as the rescue of Ustasha criminals from the hand of justice with the cooperation of the Vatican, the USA and other Western countries is. Namely, the Catholic Church together with the secret services of some countries, primarily the USA and Great Britain, in the wake of the defeat of the Axis Powers and of the Ustasha Independent State of Croatia in World War II, played an extremely dark and exceptionally important role in the organization and execution of the rescue and flight abroad, primarily to North and South America, of large numbers of Ustashas, especially the high-ranking ones, among them the leader himself, Ante Pavelic. The reasons for the rescue of the Ustashas and other Nazis and their organized smuggling through the Vatican's so-called Ratline secret channels, were concealed in the shared interest of the United States and the Vatican in their struggle against the USSR and the Communist threat in which every method was acceptable.

Beside that, the Vatican wanted to save the criminals, faithful Catholics, to whose crimes it had given its blessing during the war. The rescue of the criminals and the concealment of crimes were also a consequence of fear that if there were public exposure of the role of the Vatican and Pope Pius XII in World War II crimes, the

Communists could sieze power in elections in some predominantly Catholic countries in Europe where they already had strong support after the war, especially in France and Italy. These criminals were later used for the purpose of weakening communist countries in Europe and carrying out terrorist activities. The efforts of the Vatican to have the closest possible ties to the United States, the principal Western victorious power in World War II, were a success in the early 1980s, when at a meeting between the Pope and Reagan it was leaked that they had discussed the solutions that were adopted at Yalta in 1945. Following that, there were a series of meetings held in the presence of their associates in the course of which firm ties were established, which Richard Allen, the White House security adviser, described as one of the greatest secret alliances of all times. There is a book by Carl Bernstein....

JUDGE PATRICK ROBINSON: Mr. Milosevic, the Chamber has allowed you some latitude in making your statement. That is consistent with the practice in this Tribunal, but you have to be careful. It is questionable whether a lot of what you are saying is relevant to the case, and certainly it would not be admissible as evidence. But a broad historical sweep is, to a certain extent, permissible in an opening statement, but you must discipline yourself, particularly if you want us to favorably consider your request for additional time. Proceed.

PRESIDENT SLOBODAN MILOSEVIC: The nature of this secret alliance is described by Professor Smilja Avramov in her book *Opus Dei*, where she states the following: "Although the three ardent Catholics, Brzezinski, Casey and Walters, prepared the ground for the alliance, bearing in mind the imperatives of Roman Catholicism, and although President Regan appointed Roman Catholic activists to the most prominent positions in his administration, for example Alexander Haig, whose brother was a bishop, it would be wrong to claim that the Roman Catholic religion was the decisive factor in the policy of the United Sates in that period. The administration of the United States did not see in the alliance an expression of religion but the power of the church as an institution placed in the context of real politics. Washington used the Holy See in the same way that it would try to do somewhat later with Islam. Through this alliance, the geopolitical map of the world was reshaped and the manner of conduct of foreign policy was altered. A new, aggressive political-clerical block was created as the determining factor in United States foreign policy, which would have the most fatal consequences in relation to Yugoslavia." The words I just quoted by this scholar about the key role of the Holy See in the changes in the world were confirmed by Michael Gorbachev, who said in *La Stampa* on March 3, 1992: "Everything that happened in Eastern Europe over the past few years would not have been possible without Pope John Paul II."

Over these past few years in Eastern Europe, Yugoslavia was broken up in bloodshed; it is a state whose creation the Vatican sought to prevent during World War I, a state in whose destruction, accompanied by much bloodshed, [the Vatican] took part in once before, when it supported Hitler, the Ustasha state and the crimes the Ustasha committed during World War II. The Vatican's policy toward Serbia had already been formulated, as is evident from the 1914 letter just quoted, which dates back to a time before the creation of Yugoslavia.

After the Kingdom of the Serbs, Croats and Slovenes was created, this multi-religious state was considered to be the main barrier to the spread of Catholicism to the East. The Balkans represented for the Vatican a territory where missionary action was a priority. That is why the policy of Pope John Paul II and the Catholic Church toward Yugoslavia at the time represented the final phase of the Catholic Church's participation in the process of the destruction of Yugoslavia. I will skip a series of examples and meetings from 1991 and 1992, which confirm this, because time does not permit me to quote them all, but I will include this in the text which I will submit.

Following the recognition of Slovenia and Croatia, and then of Bosnia and Herzegovina, the Vatican at once adopted a peace-making policy. In 1994, the Pope expressed the desire to visit Zagreb, Belgrade and Sarajevo. But Vatican diplomacy did not condemn the expulsions in Operations Flash and Storm of Serbs from their lands in Croatia where they had lived for centuries. I will remind you that Lord Owen called Operation Storm "the greatest ethnic cleansing in the territory of the former Yugoslavia."

The Vatican called those actions retrieving terrain, even though this is the territory where the Serbs had lived for centuries. On October 19, 1995, the Pope said that in certain situations the use of force is not ruled out, to the extent that it is necessary for the defense of the justified rights of a people. In such situations, we are talking about a "humanitarian intervention" in order to protect human lives. But, no human lives were endangered at that time, nor were there any attacks from the UN protected zones in Krajina on the surrounding areas. This is in contrast, for example, to the protected zone in Srebrenica from which attacks were conducted for all those years when hundreds of Serbian villages were razed and the population slaughtered. A retired chaplain in the United States Army, Colonel Bigler said in Pittsburgh that the Vatican is to blame for all the troubles that occurred in Yugoslav territory and that he personally saw the bank accounts of the Vatican confirming that the Catholic Church, together with the German government, destabilized Yugoslavia and caused a decade of bloody events. Bigler claims that the Vatican pumped in millions of dollars to separatists in Yugoslavia and that the Catholic Church was very active in the events in Croatia and Slovenia.

It is well known that the Vatican and the press supported the Albanian demonstrations in Kosovo and Metohija in 1989. The archbishops in Ljubljana and Zagreb did the same. On his visit to Albania in 1994, the Pope supported the demands of the Albanian secessionists in Kosovo and Metohija. The Pope was the first one to call for energetic action against Serbia in 1998. Then he again turned into a peacemaker first on March 30, 1999, when he called a meeting of ambassadors of NATO member countries and the Security Council in order to take the initiative to stop the war against Yugoslavia. On April 1 [the Pope] wrote a letter to [President] Clinton to stop the bombing during the Easter holidays. Bearing in mind all the Vatican's activities that relate to the break-up of Yugoslavia, the message of March 12, 2000, sounds frightfully deceptive, when the Pope said: "We cannot but admit the betrayal of the Gospels committed by our brothers, especially in the second millennium. Acknowledging the sins of the past leads to the awakening of our consciousness and to compromise in the present."

Reminding us of the Pope's pledge for forgiveness of the sins of the Catholic Church, Professor Smilja Avramov recalls in her book, *Opus Dei*, critical reactions to this statement, emphasizing the following words of Leo Lyndaker, a Dutch Catholic thinker: "The Pope expressed regret for what was done in the past, but there are no indications that he is thinking about changing his behavior in the present."

The Role of the United States

As far as the United States is concerned, it has its own interests in Southeastern Europe and the former Yugoslavia. The mutual antagonisms and conflicts, the impoverishment and total inability to function independently on the political, economic or any other plane, of statelets or quasi-statelets created from the territory of the former Socialist Federal Republic of Yugoslavia, provide a most favorable ground for establishing an American political, economic and especially military presence in Europe. This last one is of particular importance for the United States, since after the break-up of the Warsaw Pact, the American military presence in West European countries lost every rationale and justification. So it is not surprising that the United States has been active in establishing this sorry situation in which the majority of these small Balkan states find themselves. In addition, after the break-up of the Eastern Bloc, some kind of a Cold War has continued in the form of preventing in every possible way the survival of a society which could serve as an example of a successful alternative to the current simple grafting of the capitalist model, which itself has problems. In that sense, Yugoslavia was not to be permitted to survive the Warsaw Pact because it would offer to Eastern European countries an uncomfortable example of independent development and an alternative to unquestioning acceptance of the values of the West, thus posing an obstacle to the New World Order shaped by the United States as the only remaining superpower in the world, in other words, the obstacle to the transformation of the world into a corporate society under the leadership of New York-based banks, where plunder is the principal motivating force.

It is well known that the United States Congress in March 1990 adopted a foreign operations law, curtailing all assistance to Yugoslavia except for the democratic parties. This act included neo-Nazis, Islamic fundamentalists and later on Albanian terrorists, who were Albanian separatists all along, among democratic parties to be assisted. It is also well known that the role of the privatized part of the American army, called MPRI, was to train the Croatian and Muslim army, and it played a key role in the offensive against the Krajina. That also confirmed that American actions in relation to the Yugoslav crisis had as their aim the maintenance of an American military presence in the Balkans through NATO, which was realized in Bosnia-Herzegovina, in Kosovo and in Macedonia, and the dominant influence of the USA and NATO in all of Europe. Economic interest, as an interest that stands above all others, it seems to me, need not even be mentioned.

The aspiration for domination is the only explanation for some at first glance irrational actions taken by the U.S., such as influencing

Alija Izetbegovic to withdraw his signature on the Cutileiro Plan[22] and also, what is less well known, the American undermining of later peace negotiations, such as the Vance-Owen and Owen-Stoltenberg plans, as well as other peace plans. It is obvious that it was not in the interest of the USA to have peace in the Balkans until the military presence of the USA and NATO was ensured and conditions were created to develop a solution under American patronage. This same aspiration is confirmed by the American insistence at the Rambouillet conference on the military presence of NATO throughout Yugoslav territory, a demand whose obvious aim was the occupation of Kosovo, the occupation of all of Yugoslavia, and ensuring the lasting presence of NATO in this region. With that goal, the administration of Bill Clinton got involved in dangerous liaisons and alliances with Islamic fundamentalist organizations and individuals, organizations such as Hezbollah, al Qaeda, the KLA[23] terrorist organization in Kosovo, and others. It is precisely those individuals and organizations that, after September 11, 2001, came to be considered the greatest threat to the USA and the Western World in general.

The price that has to be paid for this criminal policy of the Clinton Administration is enormous, and it has to be paid, unfortunately, by innocent citizens throughout the world, including American citizens, but others too, like Spaniards, et cetera. However, if the aspirations and objectives of Germany and the Vatican and the USA in the Yugoslav crisis were more or less clear and evident, what is shocking is the behavior of other members of the European Community, later on the European Union. Especially shocking were the changes in their positions under the influence of Germany, which took place in spite of the declaration of the European Community that, and I quote, "a united and democratic Yugoslavia has the best prospect of fitting into a new Europe."

The Role of the "International Community"

Even after Slovenia and Croatia were recognized and the armed conflict flared up, the European parliament, in Strasbourg in 1991, adopted a Resolution on Yugoslavia, which did not support the unilateral secession of these two Yugoslav republics. And the Council of Ministers of the European Community and the European Council also supported the territorial integrity of Yugoslavia. A wider European, that is Euro-American, forum did the same. The Council of ministers of the OSCE[24] at their meeting in Berlin in

June 1991 adopted a Declaration expressing, among other things, its support for the unity and territorial integrity of Yugoslavia. The territorial integrity of the country was especially emphasized in line with Helsinki. That a similar position at that moment in time prevailed on the other side of the Atlantic is supported by a statement by U.S. Secretary of State [James] Baker that the United States supported a united and democratic Yugoslavia and that its future should be ensured by agreement. Baker then particularly pointed out that the USA would not recognize one-sided acts of secession.

Nevertheless, the European Community, an organization that came into being as a result of a progressive process in Europe and the world, opted at the end of 1991 to support a clearly retrograde process, that is the secession of Slovenia and Croatia and of other republics. On December 17, 1991, it adopted a declaration on the criteria for recognizing the newly established states in Eastern Europe and the Soviet Union, and a declaration about Yugoslavia, calling upon all Yugoslav republics to submit requests for recognition, including proof that they have met the criteria for recognition, by December 23. In this fashion, the European Community not only trampled its own position with respect to its declaration of March 26, 1991, but also its document adopted only one month earlier and released in Rome on November 8, 1991, stating that requests for recognition of independence put forth by those republics who wish to do so may only be considered in the context of an over-all solution.

However, while the role of Germany in changing the position of the twelve European states is clear, it is not only surprising but also shocking that eleven established states would permit themselves to be coerced into doing something to which they initially in principle did not agree, under the pressure of only one out of twelve states of the European Community, however great the influence and power of that state.

Naumann, whom I have already mentioned, spoke of the concept of German domination in the region of Central Europe by breaking up that space and creating small, obedient states that he called satellites. Of course, when creating satellites, Naumann did not think of the West. However, the German *Diktat* that had to do with the secession of the Yugoslav republics and their recognition was imposed upon the European Community members by Germany, even though the *Diktat* and bowing before it were contrary to the conceptions and principles of those states, even their very own interests. All this points to the shocking fact that the member states of the European Community, including some former great powers, stooped to the level of German satellites because of the opportunism and cowardice of their incompetent leaders. Their involvement in a series of NATO military operations, including the aggression against Yugoslavia, demonstrated that they had become satellites of the USA as well.

So no one may call into question the right of Yugoslavia to survive, and no one may call into question the illegal character of its break-up as the basis and reason for the conflict. In all of this, it is cynical, to say the least, that those who reduced the peoples of Yugoslavia to internecine wars and a cycle of violence and hatred, are now pretending to be naïve, and permit themselves to administer justice. Our peoples must never forget who the main culprit is for the tragedy that took place in former Yugoslavia, and that will be clearly shown.

In Nuremberg, the first and basic crime was the crime against peace, which is not the case before this illegal Tribunal of yours, because, if it were, those who had established this unlawful institution would have to first and foremost put themselves on trial. When looking at historical developments, it is not difficult to prove — since there exist documents and records for all of this which the opposing side has — that nationalism in the territory of the former Yugoslavia did not spring from Serbia, nor from the Serbian people nor from the Serbian leadership, but primarily from the ultra-right wing separatist movements in Croatia, in Kosovo and Metohija, and in Bosnia-Herzegovina, from the Ustasha and neo-Nazis, Islamic fundamentalists and Albanian terrorists. It is not hard to prove, and you will see how this becomes clear, that the fratricidal war in the territory of the former Yugoslavia was instigated and supported militarily by the West, precisely those who have established this classic court: Germany, the Vatican and the USA, who have carried out the destruction and the break-up of a sovereign state against national and international law.

Also, it is not difficult to prove that in the break-up of Yugoslavia they resorted to undemocratic methods, contrary to their relentless claims about being very humane. They call themselves "the international community," but in the territory of the former Yugoslavia, in Croatia, Kosovo and Metohija and Bosnia-Herzegovina, they supported a totalitarian chauvinist elite, terrorists, Islamic fundamentalists and neo-Nazis whose objective was the creation of ethnically pure states, that is, states without any Serbs. The methods of cleansing the Serbian people, which the Croatian ultra-nationalist movement carried out in the beginning of the 1990s through their paramilitary units, are very similar to the methods applied to the same people in the same area fifty years earlier. In the early 1990s, it was the Serbs who were killed and expelled from Croatia, and this happed just before Tudjman came to power. It was also Serbs who were being killed and expelled from Kosovo and Metohija.

This "international community," headed by the USA, favored and actively supported Islamic fundamentalism in Bosnia-Herzegovina and Kosmet,[25] where Islamic fundamentalists carried out many crimes against the Serbs. On top of all of this, crimes against Serbs are committed in Kosmet with the full assistance of the NATO-led coalition, trampling Resolution 1244 of the Security Council which defined the terms of the cease-fire offered to Yugoslavia. When Yugoslavia could not be conquered and when the war had to be stopped, terms were offered that guaranteed the sovereignty and the territorial integrity of Yugoslavia, facilitated the arrival in Kosovo of the United Nations Protection Force responsible for protecting the entire population, and also, for providing to a limited extent for the return of the army and the police of the Yugoslav state and of Serbia to Kosovo. None of this was actually accomplished. Everything else was accomplished. NATO soldiers came hand in hand with the criminals. They expelled hundreds of thousands of people, killed thousands and torched many churches, but I will discuss this later.

What I wish to say now is that, as far as crimes against the Serbian people are concerned over the past ten years, there is enormous and detailed documentation that was offered to this institution from many different institutions throughout the world. The opposing side did not even glance at these documents. The reason is that this "international community," when causing conflict in our territory, decided in advance that the Serbs were to be blamed for everything and that is why all others could and had to be portrayed as victims. As to how the war started in the territory of the former Yugoslavia, the authors of the so-called Kosovo indictment against me, in paragraphs 79 and 80 presented one of their rare truthful assertions in this otherwise totally false and shameful document. I am quoting their text: "Slovenia on June 25, 1991, proclaimed independence from the SFRY, which led to the outbreak of war." This is what it says in their document. And also: "Croatia proclaimed its independence on June 25, 1991, which led to fighting between the Croatian military forces on the one hand and the JNA and paramilitary units and the army of the Serbian Krajina on the other hand. Bosnia and Herzegovina proclaimed its independence on March 6, 1992, which after April 6, 1992, led to war of wide proportions."

So even the authors of this false indictment, who probably did not envisage that they would issue indictments against me for Croatia and Bosnia later on, themselves stated who caused the war in the former Yugoslavia. The participants in this enterprise, which most certainly is criminal (and it concerns both foreign and domestic actors), acted in violation of Yugoslav law and international law. By trampling the law and executing the forceful secession of Slovenia, Croatia and Bosnia-Herzegovina, they committed the gravest of all crimes, such as those who were tried in Nuremberg and in Tokyo under the jurisdiction of the legal and permanent International Criminal Court, and that is the crime against peace.

Illegal Secessions

In contrast to the authorities of Slovenia and Croatia, and the Islamic-Croatian authorities in Bosnia-Herzegovina, who carried out armed secessions, and in contrast to their instigators and helpers from Germany, Austria and the Vatican, and later on from the USA and from the NATO pact, the Serbian people and the Serbian leadership, and I personally strove to preserve the Yugoslav state. By doing this, we were on the side of the law, whereas the destroyers of Yugoslavia were violating national and international law. They were invoking the right to self-determination but this was only a smokescreen to hide the essence of their criminal acts of unlawful and violent secession, because the Yugoslav peoples and especially the Yugoslav republics did not have the right to one-sided secession from the Yugoslav state, neither according to the constitution of Yugoslavia, nor according to the constitutions of those republics, nor according to international law. In particular, they did not have the right to achieve this objective by force, over the dead bodies of their fellow citizens and the federal state. Article 5 of the Constitution of Yugoslavia of 1974, which was in force then, states: "The territory of the Socialist Federal Republic of Yugoslavia is a unified territory and is composed of the territories of the republics. The borders of the SFRY cannot be changed without the agreement of all the republics and the autonomous provinces."

It follows unmistakably from this that no single republic or nationality within the SFRY had the unilateral right to secede from the SFRY or to sever any part of its territory. This was possible only on the basis of the agreement of all. Bearing this in mind and bearing in mind the desire expressed in Slovenia and Croatia, and later in Bosnia-Herzegovina and in Macedonia to leave the Yugoslav Federation and, the Serbian side, in an attempt to avoid any kind of conflict as confirmed by witness Borislav Jovic, the former president of the Presidency of Yugoslavia, beginning in August 1990, tried to convince the representatives of other republics in the Federal bodies to adopt a law that would regulate the right of self-determination appropriately. But, as Jovic says in his book, which was quoted here, these other republics were determined to follow this through to the end, even at the cost of incidents and conflict. Let me remind you of Tudjman's speech, which was quoted here, where he says: "There would have been no war had Croatia not wanted it."

Yes, without such a war no one would have been able to expel half a million Serbs from territories which they had inhabited for centuries, people who at the time of Croatian secession were not asking for a state but merely for autonomy, people who, up to that point, were a constituent people according to the Croatian Constitution. Croatia proclaimed its independence through secession from Yugoslavia by breaking the Constitution and using force. This was an illegal, armed and violent secession. And an illegal, armed and violent secession leading to tens of thousands of people killed is crime under Yugoslav national law and international law, just as aiding and abetting such a bloody war is a crime.

The foreign participants — and those are the same ones who are behind this illegal court, the purpose of which is to grant amnesty to them and to shift the blame onto the victims, and victims could be found among all Yugoslav peoples — aided the secessions of the former Yugoslav republics in a way that was not permissible under international law. That the situation regarding the secession of the former Yugoslav republics is precisely so was explicitly confirmed by Antonio Cassese, the former president of this institution in a monograph he wrote.[26] On pages 269 and 270, he pointed out that the Yugoslav republics did not have the right to self-determination, either under international law or under Yugoslav national law. As in the case of the twelve Soviet republics, the six Yugoslav republics did not have the right to self-determination under international law. This right was not provided for in the Yugoslav Constitution either, since, unlike the Soviet Constitution, the Yugoslav Constitution did not contain clauses that granted the republics the right to secede.

Therefore, just as this illegal Prosecution, in paragraphs 79 and 80 of the so-called Kosovo indictment, in a moment of inattention pointed out who caused the war in the former Yugoslavia, the former president of this illegal court, at the time when he was head of this institution, in the same book on page 273, after having established the illegality of the secession, drew an identical conclusion, identical to the one that the Prosecution inadvertently slipped into the referenced paragraphs. That conclusion reads: "It is well known that in Croatia and in Bosnia and Herzegovina as in several former Soviet republics the secession revived the ancient hatreds and led to terrible bloodshed."

This is well known to anyone who has a minimum of honesty and wishes to accept that which is obvious and true. One who does not have that minimum of honesty may permit himself to distort obvious and well known facts, and to twist them into their opposites, except when the truth inadvertently slips out. Nevertheless, it must not be forgotten that to have the truth as an ally is a firm guarantee of victory sooner or later. Having the truth as an adversary is a certain path to humiliating defeat.

All that I am saying here is the truth about the bloody break-up of Yugoslavia, an internationally recognized state, which had the legal right to survive, just as it did according to morality and historical facts, and, most importantly, in the best interests and well-being of its citizens. Time does not permit me to present even some indispensable facts and conclusions. I hope that you will not oppose, in the case of Kosovo, accepting the seven "white books" from the Yugoslav government as part of the material that has been entered into evidence, and all the documentation which has been submitted to the regular and legal International Court of Justice in The Hague pertaining to the aggression against Yugoslavia. Later, I will submit other documents as well.

In relation to Kosovo, I now wish to emphasize several things which, with hindsight, will show how exact and correct Yugoslavia's approach was. Now everyone can see what happened and what the consequences are.

The Drama of Kosovo

Five thousand acts of terrorism were perpetrated in Kosovo in only the first year of the foreign presence in Kosovo and Metohija, beginning from the moment the Yugoslav army and the Serbian police withdrew from this Serbian province in June 1999. Several thousand people were killed or abducted. One hundred and fifty churches were destroyed.

Gentlemen, had one hundred and fifty mosques or Catholic churches or synagogues been demolished anywhere else, the whole world would be talking about it. All these crimes were committed under the auspices and protection of the United Nations, trampling UN resolutions, and transforming the security forces of the United Nations into occupation forces in collaboration with Albanian terrorists. Over 300,000 inhabitants were expelled under the auspices of the United Nations and in collaboration with them.

On the other hand, more than 200,000 Albanians, foreign citizens, moved into Kosovo, mainly from Albania and Macedonia. Persecution of all non-Albanians, especially all Serbs, has continued with undiminished fervor and continues to this very day. Even though there is a decline in the volume and scale of the consequences of such criminal hysteria, it is because almost everything that is Serbian and non-Albanian has already been cleansed from Kosovo. In that southern province of the Republic of Serbia, there were very few left that could awaken that collective thirst for violence, but even that small number of non-Albanians and Serbs remaining in Kosmet was too much for chauvinistic Albanian terrorists, and it culminated in a new wave of anti-Serbian violence. Right now, Kosmet has been practically cleansed of all Serbs after the most recent efforts made by witness Halid Barani, who testified here on March 17 of this year. He, of course, is not the only criminal who was brought here to testify. Numerous other criminals have testified here. But it has been proven that Halid, with his invented story of the alleged Serbian crimes against three Albanian boys who drowned in a river while allegedly fleeing from their Serbian persecutors, gave the signal, the green light for a hysterical mass assault on everything Serbian, for which KFOR arrested him. Another witness here, Shukri Buja, another criminal and terrorist, confirmed here that he was in command of a KLA unit in Racak and that he was the first, together with his like-minded criminal followers, to open fire with a machine gun on the policemen who were approaching the village. This recent pogrom, like the earlier pogroms against the non-Albanian population in Kosovo and Metohija, is the result of a joint criminal enterprise between this institution and its witnesses, whose interests are defended here.

Those who support this most retrograde movement engendered in Europe in modern history collaborate with such witnesses. Bearing in mind what happened in Croatia and Bosnia-Herzegovina, especially the more than evident continuity between the separatist and nationalistic tendencies and movements and their pro-Nazi and extremist leaders from World War II, and further bearing in mind the irrational fervor — even passion — with which this so-called Prosecution tries to support and justify the acts of those who persist in revising the results of two world wars in order to achieve what they failed to achieve because they had been defeated in those wars, a very troubling conclusion emerges: the joint criminal enterprise, in which this institution is a participant, is far broader [as measured by] the number of participants, by the criminal plan, and by the time span and the territory involved.

Today many in the West are trying to explain and justify the violence perpetrated by the terrorists in Kosovo by saying that it is revenge for the long-term terror and repression of the Albanian population in Kosovo and Metohija. This is a lie. Where are these terrorized, persecuted, arrested, killed Albanians from all those years? Such arguments are not only based on falsified facts, but they cannot hold water in the face of the irrefutable fact of the historical continuity of the persecution of the Serbian and Christian population in general in the territory of Kosovo and Metohija from the time of the Turkish occupation, with sporadic pauses, to the present day, although there were no real interruptions to speak of. The ethnic cleansing of the Serbs from Kosovo and Metohija has a long history.

It intensified significantly after the founding in Prizren in 1878 of the so-called Albanian League, which drafted the idea of creating a Greater Albania. Konstantin Jiricek, the eminent European historian, maintains that 150,000 Serbs were expelled from the Old Serbia (from Kosovo) between 1878 and 1912; this amounted to a quarter of the Serbian population. In addition to many Russian, French and other sources, there is rich British diplomatic documentation that deals with this process, for example, the letters of Sir George Banham from 1901, in which he speaks about the expulsion of Serbs and large numbers of Serbian families, but I have no time to quote them right now.

The development of the situation in Kosovo and Metohija over the course of the twentieth century has shown that nothing has changed in the methods of de-Serbianizing that space. On the contrary, the Albanian policy of pressure and terror against the Serbs and Montenegrins became even worse and far more perilous. This became particularly evident during World War I, especially during the withdrawal of Serbian troops through Albania in 1915. There are numerous documents concerning this. When, at the beginning of World War II, Italy created the puppet Greater Albania, which included most of Kosovo and Metohija, it was a new opportunity for terror against the non-Albanian, primarily Serbian population, as evidenced by the unequivocal statement of Mustafa Kroja, Prime Minister of the puppet Albanian government in June 1941, and I quote: "Maximum efforts have to be made to expel all the Serb old-timers in Kosovo and take them to concentration camps in Albania. The Serb newcomers have to be killed."

Recalling the statement made by this Fascist Prime Minister, historian Slavenko Terzic points out that according to the documents of the American Special Services, Albanian nationalists killed 10,000 Serbs and expelled 100,000 people from the beginning of the war in April 1941 to August 1942. A similar number of Albanians moved from Albania to Kosovo.

Herman Neubacher, special envoy of the Third Reich to southeastern Europe wrote in the autumn of 1943: "The Albanians have accelerated persecutions. I urgently recommended to the [Albanian] government to stop the expulsions. When I saw that my intervention did not produce any results, I asked to resign from my mission in Albania." And this is written by an envoy of the Third Reich, a Nazi. Even he was horrified by this.

Prior Makarije, on April 3, 1968, wrote to the Serbian Patriarch German about persecutions of the Serbs because the Yugoslav authorities after World War II concealed this from the public, especially from the public outside of Kosovo. He says: "The Albanians are again showing their historic hatred toward the Serbs and we find ourselves in a situation more difficult than during the Austrian or Turkish eras. Then, at least, we had some rights. Violence is an everyday occurence, thefts are taking place in broad daylight, and insults and threats. You certainly hear from others what is happening to the Serbs in Kosmet. The Department of Internal Affairs in the Province in 1966 says that: 'In high schools — gymnasiums and teachers' secondary schools — nationalism is legally taught to the youth.' Hostile activity is growing and, as of late, there is more and more of such activity. Physical attacks against the people of Montenegrin and Serbian nationality are taking place daily. Hostile threats and openly hostile public speeches are being made in public places." Thus writes the Prior to the Patriarch.

The Russian Balkans expert, Professor Elena Guskova, says in her book, *The History of the Yugoslav Crisis from 1990 to 2000*, on page 44 that: "Demonstrations in the Province are accompanied by acts of sabotage in factories, the distribution of leaflets, and measures to turn Kosmet into an ethically clean province. The chauvinists have used all sorts of methods and threaten the outright extermination of Serbs and Montenegrins. They have been desecrating cultural monuments and Orthodox cemeteries, burning houses, killing people, seizing others' land by force, and limiting freedom of movement. The consequence of this has been the massive departure of Serbian families from this province. Of 1,451 settlements in 1981, there were no Serbs left in 635 of them. There are only 216 Serbian villages that are still left there. During these ten years, Albanian terrorism was very hard to restrain, so that by 1991 less than ten percent of the Serbs remained in Kosmet."

Thus, the term "ethnic cleansing" and "ethnically clean" first appeared and began to be used in connection with these events. And your witness here, the Slovenian professor of constitutional law, Ivan Kristan, says in an article entitled "The Constitutional Status of Autonomous Provinces of the SFRY," published in 1981, I call your attention to that, in 1981, and I am quoting from this article: "The Albanian nationalist concept of an ethnically pure republic of Kosovo and the unification of all Albanians into one republic negates one of the basic achievements of the National Liberation Struggle.[27] The motto of ethnically cleansed Kosovo offers, instead of equality and unity of nations and nationalities,[28] constant tabulation of their numbers and chauvinism." This was cited in 1981 by a constitutional expert, a Slovenian professor whom you yourselves have brought here. I continue to quote him: "Numerous pressures are being exerted and chauvinist excesses [committed] against other nations and nationalities; this has gone so far that members of certain nations are beginning to move out because they feel threatened. This has been going on for a while in Kosovo, from where a considerable number of Serbs and Montenegrins have moved out, so that according to the census of 1981 in comparison to the one in 1971, there are fewer members of these two nations in relative terms and in absolute numbers than before."

JUDGE PATRICK ROBINSON: Mr. Milosevic, before you continue, we are going to take a break now for 20 minutes, and we will sit, with the cooperation of the interpreters, until 2:00 p.m. So we are adjourned for 20 minutes.

Recess taken at 12:20 p.m.

On resuming at 12:43 p.m.

JUDGE PATRICK ROBINSON: Please continue, Mr. Milosevic.

PRESIDENT SLOBODAN MILOSEVIC: Mr. Robinson, I insist that you allocate some time for me for tomorrow.

JUDGE PATRICK ROBINSON: We will consider that near to the end of today's session.

PRESIDENT SLOBODAN MILOSEVIC: Very well. I repeat. In a 1981 article, Kristan, your witness, points to a crucial link between the greater Albanian Fascist movement from World War II, the so-called Balists and the separatist Albanian movement of the 1980s. It is the same movement and the same participants, who, at the end of the twentieth century, developed into naked terrorism. It intended to ethnically cleanse this cradle of Serbian civilization of Serbs and other non-Albanian people once and for all with secessionist motives and by terrorist means, in cooperation with the aggressor force of nineteen NATO countries. Kristan writes in that article about this link and about the continuity of greater Albanian Fascists from World War II: "The irredentist aspirations of the Albanian nationalists in Kosovo are not recent. They actually appear as an extension of various Quisling and Fascist organizations."

Albanian Separatism

The words and deeds coming from Albania as well as from Kosovo and Metohija demonstrate that the greater Albanian aspirations and territorial pretensions of Albania did not wither with the defeat of the greater Albanian movement in World War II, together with the German and Italian Nazis and Fascists.

Thus, the General Secretary of the Albanian Communist Party, Enver Hoxha, wrote in a letter to the Central Committee of the Soviet Communist Party in 1949, relying on the conflict between Yugoslavia and Stalin, and I quote: "The Congress of Berlin and the Versailles Peace Treaty unjustly harmed the interests of Albania and the Albanian national minorities in Kosovo. They do not agree with that resolution of this question and they do not wish to remain within the borders of Yugoslavia, regardless of its political structure. Their only ideal is to join Albania."

The aforementioned Russian historian Elena Guskova says in her voluminous book that: "The separatist activity of the radically minded part of Albanians in Kosovo and Metohija started immediately after World War II and has not been interrupted for one moment. Already by 1965, the security services discovered in the Province several groups which had infiltrated Kosmet several years earlier from Albania in order to create illegal national organizations. At the end of the 1950s and in the early 1960s an organization of the revolutionary movement for the unification of Albanians was active in Kosmet and was headed by Adem Demaci."

The same author, after having demonstrated that Albanian terror over the course of the 1960s became much more active, meaning that Albanian separatists had in that period organized "provocations, sabotages, the desecration of churches and Serbian cultural monuments, and threatened the Orthodox population," explains that the situation did not calm down even in the 1970s, despite the fact that in 1974 Kosmet was practically withdrawn from the legal system of the Republic of Serbia, and cites an interview given by a leading official of the Yugoslav police, the federal minister of internal affairs at the time, a Croat, by the way, Franjo Herljevic, who presented the following information, and I quote: "The security organs discovered over 1,000 people who were involved in undermining the state from the position of Albanian nationalism from 1974 until the beginning of 1981." Many of them were linked to one of the most active organizations, the so-called Red Front. This is a pro-Albanian organization active in the territory of Western countries which is directed and channeled by the Albanian Labor Party.

The Albanian separatist movement, starting with the unrest of Albanian separatists in March 1981, openly advocated the idea of the Kosovo Republic, that is the secession of Kosovo from Serbia and then from Yugoslavia, and finally joining this territory to Albania.

If you look at the demographic structure of Kosovo and Metohija at the end of the 19th century, and then at the end of the 20th century, you can see that it drastically changed to the detriment of the Serbs. The biggest changes took place specifically during World War II from 1941 to 1945, when crimes were taking place there.

Political, judicial and executive power in Kosovo and Metohija was in the hands of the Albanian national minority in Serbia after the adoption of the 1974 Constitution. Particularly, from 1966, and then, of course, after the adoption of the 1974 Constitution, the Albanians in this part of Serbia used this power to harass the Serbian majority and to inflame inter-ethnic intolerance, which resulted in daily expulsions of Serbs, instead of in the essential spirit of tolerance and understanding and civilized relations between the two peoples.

The paradox of this whole situation lies in the fact that the Albanians in Kosmet, whose leaders claimed that they had been discriminated against and oppressed for centuries, actually achieved such a level of economic prosperity that already by the 1980s one could see a vast difference between the situation in Kosovo and the situation in Albania, where they had their own nation state.

The Albanian minority in Serbia, namely in Kosovo and Metohija, experienced a scientific, cultural and educational rebirth, thanks chiefly to the educational system of Serbia, precisely during the period when the Serbian population in the Province was being drastically reduced. Of course, Serbian intellectuals, under such pressure, were also moving out of Kosovo. Over the course of 1981 alone, scores of doctors left the medical center in Pristina. Many university professors were forced to leave. On the other hand, Great Albanian chauvinist propaganda reached its peak from 1975 to 1980, following the adoption of the 1974 Constitution, which gave the Province the attributes of statehood.

There was practically no border between Yugoslavia and Serbia, actually between Kosovo and Metohija, and neighboring Albania. And this was during the golden era of Enver Hoxha's rule in Tirana. The Kosovo Albanian appetite for ever greater independence was growing into the first step towards secession, to the extent that the Kosovo Albanians were given ever greater rights to autonomy during the time of Tito.

The first mass demonstrations date from November 1968. It became evident that later, following the 1980s, they were no longer satisfied with broad autonomy and guaranteed political and human rights as provided under the 1974 Constitution. This was expressed in the mass rebellion of Albanian separatists in the spring of 1981 under a slogan calling for the creation of a Kosovo Republic. This is something that was also mentioned by your witness Ivan Kristan.

The influence of foreign elements which aided and abetted the break-up of Yugoslavia has been thoroughly investigated. It is precisely these influential elements that came forward with quite malicious accusations. One of these is that the crisis in Kosovo and Metohija actually started in 1989 with the adoption of the amendments to the Constitution of Serbia, which are claimed to have abolished Kosovo's autonomy and limited the human rights of Albanians.

This is a groundless accusation. The Serbian constitutional amendments of 1989 in fact established the constitutional unity of the Republic of Serbia, which up until then had been under the tutelage of its two provinces, because Kosovo and Vojvodina had, up until the adoption of those amendments, participated in the rule of the republic, but the republic did not have any influence on what was going on in the provinces. Thus, the republic could not exercise its constitutional authority in parts of its own territory, primarily to be able to care for the well being of its people. The amendments in the Republic of Serbia corrected the anomalies in the position of the Republic of Serbia in its relations to its autonomous provinces, but these amendments and the 1990 Constitution did not in any way violate or abolish the human rights of Albanians. They continued to enjoy free education and a press in their own language. And everything else: proceedings before judicial organs that they could conduct in their own language, and more protection than any other national minority in any other country.

Acts of Terrorism Committed by the KLA

The Kosovo crisis entered into a new phase with the secession of Slovenia and Croatia. The Albanian secessionists embarked upon overt terrorist attacks with the formation of the terrorist KLA. This will be demonstrated with documents that I will present here. This organization armed and trained its members with the assistance of some foreign countries, first of all Germany, the USA, Switzerland, and some Islamic states.

At the time, lists of banks and the numbers of bank accounts where contributions were sent for the KLA were published in Germany and Switzerland. But, I will not go into this because I do not have enough time.

The latest weapons delivered to the KLA via Albania were worth several million German marks according to reports in *European* and *KonKret* magazines from March 1999. OSCE observers at a checkpoint on the border between Albania and Yugoslavia were surprised to note that members of the KLA were wearing German uniforms.

Moreover, the German intelligence service admitted that it organized and trained the Albanian terrorists in Berlin and in other places and provided terrorists with transportation. Aid and assistance was also provided by Turkey, as it was by the Albanian narco mafia. This is something that is well known, and we have quite reliable sources for these facts.

The main task of arming these forces was assumed by the American intelligence service with the assistance of the British [secret] service. According to *The Scotsman*, the American intelligence service contacted MI5 in order to train the KLA, and then MI5 or MI6 passed this task on to certain British military companies, which in turn performed that task. They published lists of weapons and other equipment, but I have no time to speak about that today.

The most frequent targets of KLA activities were police stations and military institutions and initially also the civilian population. Their victims were very often their own people just because they were loyal citizens of Serbia. The terrorist activities were increasing from year to year.

A vast number of attacks took place, but I will mention only a few. In a report for 1998, from January 1 to December 31, there were 1,129 terrorist acts in which 216 members of the Ministry of Internal Affairs were killed, 115 were wounded, and 187 suffered minor injuries, while many were kidnapped. There were 755 terrorist attacks and provocations against the civilian population, in which 173 citizens had been killed, including 46 Serbs and Montenegrins, 77 Albanians, three Romas, two Muslims, and 42 unidentified persons. As the numbers show, the KLA killed more Albanians that Serbs.

In that year, the terrorists abducted 292 civilian citizens, of which 173 were Serbs and Montenegrins, 100 Albanians, fourteen Roma, one Muslim, one Bulgarian, one Greek and one Macedonian. Of those, they killed 31, nine escaped, and 142 are still missing.

Then further explanations are given with respect to all [the weapons] that were used: mortars, hand-held rocket launchers, explosive devices, anti-tank mines, and so on. All of this happened at the time when Ibrahim Rugova claimed that the KLA was just a figment of the imagination, which was created by Serb propaganda and did not really exist.

This information is sufficiently clear, and I wonder if any government in the world would have remained passive when confronted with such terrorist activities. It is understandable that the police not only had to react to terrorist attacks but it was necessary for them to take action to neutralize and combat terrorist groups in order to re-establish control.

Attacks against the army are something that you know very well, and the public knows too. There has been a misconception in a broad spectrum of views within different international political structures, particularly in the area of international public opinion, especially since 1998, that the KLA was some kind of liberation movement, which is totally unfounded. For example, the

Federation of American Scientists, which is considered to be a think-tank, published a report in 1998 in which it states that the KLA terrorists came from known terrorist organizations in the world. According to the FAS report, the State Department is the only institution in the USA that deals with the question of terrorist organizations seriously.

John Pike, the first security head of FAS stated that his organization had developed a detailed study which analyzed the entire structure of the KLA, as opposed to the State Department. According to him, KLA tactics consist of ambushes. Its members are organized in cells of three to five persons, which is characteristic of terrorist organizations. Members of the groups are visibly obsessed with the idea of secession from Yugoslavia and unification with Albania. They carry out orders without protest. In the ranks of the KLA there are thousands of mercenaries from Saudi Arabia, Albania, Bosnia-Herzegovina and Croatia, as well as from Western countries.

Training camps on the territory of Albania are also listed. The FAS report also points out that the long-term KLA objective is to unite the Albanian population in Kosovo, Albania and Macedonia into a Greater Albania. The position of all police forces in the Western countries is that the KLA represents a classic terrorist organization, with all its characteristics, because they are all aware of the links this organization has to drug dealers and white slave traders.

The U.S. special envoy to the Balkans, [Robert] Gelbard, stated at a press conference in Belgrade on February 23, 1998, and I quote: "We are deeply disturbed and we most strongly condemn the impermissible violence carried out by terrorist groups in Kosovo, especially the KLA. There is no doubt that this is a terrorist group. I do not accept any kind of justification. Having worked on the subject of terrorist activity for years, I know very well how to recognize and define a terrorist group, and I base this on facts, not on any kind of rhetoric. The activities of this group speak for themselves."

He called upon the Albanian leaders, and I quote: "to condemn terrorism and thus show which side they are on." Of course, nothing came of this. In the second half of 1998, the U.S. establishment outside the Clinton Administration held the unequivocal belief that the KLA was a typical terrorist organization. This is also confirmed by a carefully compiled document prepared by a Senate Committee of the Republican Party in 1999, which says, and I quote: "By the time the NATO air strikes began, the Clinton Administration's partnership with the KLA was unambiguous.... Such an effusive embrace by top Clinton Administration officials of an organization that only a year ago one of its own top officials labeled as 'terrorist' is, to say the least, a startling development. Even more importantly, the new Clinton/KLA partnership may obscure troubling allegations about the KLA that the Clinton Administration has thus far neglected to address."[29]

This is an official document of the U.S. Senate. The nature and the role of the KLA as a terrorist organization are amply documented in this transcript of the U.S. Congress for the year 2000. Frank Ciluffo, an official from a program called Globalized Organized Crime Program, revealed during testimony before the Judicial Committee of the U.S. House of Representatives on December 13, 2000, what was largely concealed from public view, namely, that the KLA raised part of its funds from the sale of narcotics.

Albania and Kosovo lie in the middle of the Balkan route which links the Golden Crescent of Afghanistan and Pakistan to the drug markets of Europe. "This route is worth an estimated US $400 million per year and handles about 80 percent of the heroin destined for Europe." This was the testimony at a hearing before a Congressional Committee. An analysis of the Resolutions of the United Nations Security Council on Kosovo and Metohija would also demonstrate that. With this money, the KLA buys the support of the United States. Hasim Taci was a guest at the Democratic National Convention in Boston. An Albanian testified here as a protected witness that he personally killed not only Serbs but Albanians too, and that he even used a knife to carve figures on the chests of the victims.

JUDGE PATRICK ROBINSON: I think the witness is protected.

PROSECUTOR GEOFFREY NICE: I am finding it a little difficult to follow exactly what the accused is saying, but I think the passage that deals with protected evidence ought probably to be protected now.

JUDGE PATRICK ROBINSON: Yes. It will be protected, and be more careful in the future, Mr. Milosevic.

PRESIDENT SLOBODAN MILOSEVIC: It is not evidence that must be protected. The witness is the one who is protected, and I did not mention the name of the witness. I am just reminding you of what the witness testified about.

Resolutions of the Security Council about Kosovo and Metohija adopted before the NATO aggression against Yugoslavia show that the Security Council believed that there were terrorist attacks in Kosovo and Metohija and that the KLA was clearly defined in these resolutions as a terrorist organization. Resolution 1160, and I quote: "condemn[s] all acts of terrorism by the Kosovo Liberation Army or any other group or individual and all external support for terrorist activity in Kosovo, including finance, arms and training." And we can see who was involved in this training.

In paragraph 2, the leadership of the Kosovo Albanians is called upon, and I quote: "to condemn all terrorist actions," and it is emphasized that all elements of the Albanian community in Kosovo should achieve their objectives only by political means. This remained a mere promise that was never fulfilled.

That this remained merely an empty promise was demonstrated later as the terrorist activities gained strength when much larger quantities of weapons were brought in and terrorist actions intensified with the engagement of the West.

Resolution 1199, and I quote: "Condemn[s] ... terrorism in pursuit of political goals by any group or individual and all external support for such activities in Kosovo, including the supplying of arms and training for terrorist activities in Kosovo."

What the Clinton Administration did, which led to what happened on September 11, is a key matter and nobody can deny that. You can see how many among those arrested are direct participants in these events. There is ample evidence to prove clearly that these people took part in the activities of the KLA in Kosovo and in Bosnia-Herzegovina, practically as members of al Qaeda.

The Security Council expressed its concern over reports of the constant violations of the ban against providing weapons to terrorists, as stated in Resolution 1160. In paragraph 6 it insisted again on the condemnation of all terrorist activities and emphasized that all members of the Albanian community should achieve their goals through peaceful means only. In paragraph 11 all countries are warned against soliciting financial resources for terrorists in their territory.

Resolution 1203 condemns terrorism by any group or individual in order to achieve political objectives and any foreign support for such activities in Kosovo, including the provision of weapons and training for terrorist activities in Kosovo. Concern is also expressed over reports of continued violations of previous resolutions. Paragraph 10 insists, and I quote, that: "the Kosovo Albanian leadership condemn all terrorist actions."

The leadership of the Kosovo Albanians, however, never condemned the terrorist actions of the KLA. In contrast to these evident facts, which clearly pointed to the terrorist character of the KLA and its activities in Kosovo and Metohija, every country has the right and duty to take all necessary measures to suppress such activities. The Clinton Administration, under the influence of the powerful Albanian lobby and its drug-related money, publicly and directly sided with this terrorist organization and became its protector from mid-1998 onwards. Therefore, it is not surprising that the [Clinton] Administration took measures to prevent the break-up of the KLA after that and to ensure it the status of a party involved in the process of negotiations for the solution of Kosovo's problems, and even brought it to Rambouillet in this capacity.

[Richard] Holbrooke,[30] together with Gelbard, the other U.S. representative, met with a group of leaders of the terrorist KLA and conducted a dialogue with them before TV cameras in a public rehabilitation of the KLA. Soon afterwards, he admitted that Gelbard had previously established contact with them.

American Intervention

Our police forces practically broke up and neutralized the KLA terrorists and their strongholds during August and September 1998. Then again, representatives from the Clinton Administration appeared on the scene. Then came a Verification Commission, whose main objective, it was later established, was to reanimate, revitalize and protect the KLA.

JUDGE O-GON KWON: Mr. Milosevic, would you hold a minute.

[Trial Chamber confers]

JUDGE PATRICK ROBINSON: Yes, continue, Mr. Milosevic.

PRESIDENT SLOBODAN MILOSEVIC: The appointment of William Walker as the leader of the Verification Commission was no accident. This was done on the insistence of the CIA, whose agent he was. It should be remembered that he had been the U.S. Ambassador in El Salvador and Nicaragua, where he served as an assistant to the well-known Colonel in charge of special operations, such as supplying arms, recruiting mercenaries and organizing death squads. The developments of the late twentieth century showed that the Clinton Administration used the Albanian nationalist and separatist movement, and other similar movements around the world, in order to achieve its interests. That is why it wholeheartedly supported such movements, most often by way of sponsored terrorism. This was also confirmed by the conclusion of the Committee for Foreign Relations of the U.S. Congress in 1992, which recommended provoking unrest in Kosovo whenever it was necessary to get concessions from Belgrade.

An analysis issued by a Republican commission of the U.S. Senate states that the NATO intervention in Kosovo and Metohija had already been planned in earnest in August 1998 by the Clinton Administration but then it lacked, and I quote: "an acceptable media event which would, in the eyes of the international community, serve as a political alibi for intervention."

There were lies piled upon lies waiting for a trigger to set events into motion. Official NATO personnel were promptly engaged in preparations for the intervention, which, in the middle of 1998 during [General Wesley] Clark's mandate, established initial contacts with the KLA. This comes from the transcript of a background briefing for the U.S. Department of Defense on July 15, 1998. These initial contacts were officially confirmed by NATO in mid-1998.

The KLA, according to many reports, had been given covert support and training since the mid-1990s by the CIA and the German secret service, the BND. NATO knew of and supported these secret operations. All this is stated in Michael Kosydowski's book, *Freedom Fighters*.

This documentation confirms that the KLA, which was initially from mid-1988 treated as a terrorist organization, established close links with NATO thanks to the decision of the Clinton Administration. This partnership prepared for the NATO aggression while conducting parallel farcical negotiations in Rambouillet.

The turning point was precisely the needed media event which was concocted on the basis of what took place in Racak. According to the well-tested scenario used in the "Markale Market" incident in Bosnia, a massacre allegedly took place in the village of Racak, and the experienced chief of the OSCE mission, Walker, called it an unprecedented crime committed by Serbian security forces. This was the climax of the preparations carried out by the OSCE mission and especially by its chief, in order to create a pretext for the NATO aggression that followed a previously developed Clinton Administration plan.

I have shown you a video of Walker's deputy testifying, in which you can see the orange jeeps of the Verification Mission on the hill overlooking Racak. You can see what really happened there on the video. You also saw that in the testimony of their commander there.

I have no time to go into this now, but I wish to quote military commentator Milovan Drecun from his book about the Racak case, *The Second Battle of Kosovo*, which states:

"The Racak case will enter many textbooks as a brilliantly executed and pure anti-terrorist action carried out by members of the police, but also as one of the most monstrous media deceptions ever seen by the world. We are witnesses of the fact that the events in Racak are still manipulated almost daily, especially in The Hague, where serious falsifications are persistently being perpetuated. It is well known that the sponsors of these events did not want it to be revealed that there was no massacre in Racak, but sought to accuse the Serbian side with this story."

JUDGE PATRICK ROBINSON: That is the commentator, Mr. Milosevic, the commentator that you just referred to, can you repeat his name?

PRESIDENT SLOBODAN MILOSEVIC: Milovan Drecun, in his book *The Second Battle of Kosovo*.

JUDGE PATRICK ROBINSON: And he is from where?

PRESIDENT SLOBODAN MILOSEVIC: Belgrade.

JUDGE PATRICK ROBINSON: Thanks.

PRESIDENT SLOBODAN MILOSEVIC: There is evidence which clearly shows that after agreement on the presence of the Verification Commission in Kosovo, over 500 terrorist KLA attacks were perpetrated from October 1998 to the end of January 1999. And in the same period, 35 villages inhabited by Serbs and Montenegrins were ethnically cleansed by using the Verification Mission as a cover. Also, in only the first 11 days of 1999, 80 terrorist attacks by the KLA were perpetrated against the police, the army and civilians. The KLA was renamed the Kosovo Protection Corps as a reward for these and all other crimes committed primarily against the Serbs but also against other non-Albanians and even against Albanians themselves, as well as for collaboration during the NATO aggression. The UN gave the KPC legitimate status, enabling it to access funds in Western countries through bilateral channels, including direct military aid. And this was taking place at the very time when it was understood that the KPC would have to disarm immediately.

This is only one detail in a sea of abuses that occurred at the time when the implementation of Security Council Resolution 1244 was expected to take place. And Agim Ceku, a notorious terrorist, was placed in charge of this Protection Force. Ceku committed many crimes against Serbs in Kosovo and Metohija as well as against Albanians, who were executed by KPC on his orders because of their loyalty to Serbia, the state in which they lived. Before that, this same Ceku fought against the Serbs in Croatia, where, as an officer of the Croatian army, he gained prominence because of the crimes he committed against the Serbs during Operation Storm and especially because of the genocide conducted against the Serbs in the Medak pocket, where women, after being raped, were doused with gasoline and set on fire.

There is available evidence about this here, but Ceku is protected. He is an ally despite the fact that he is a notorious murderer and terrorist. You could have seen, for example, in November 2003, in the Belgrade press, photographs which I have no time to use here. But you can see KLA members in uniform holding the heads of Serbs in both hands. You can also a see bag full of the heads of Serbs who had been beheaded. Everybody knows that the person who is triumphantly holding the human heads is Sadik Djuflaj from the Decani area, with his son Valon Djuflaj standing beside him. Both of them committed crimes in the Decani-Pec zone under the command of Ramus and Daut Haradinaj. And this is just a small part of what they had done.

All this information has been published, including photographs and names, but all of it is ignored. All of this is being overlooked so that this same Djuflaj, with thousands of other terrorists of the former KLA, is now a member of the Kosovo Protection Corps, holding the rank of corporal. And they have been entrusted by this so-called international community to maintain a multiethnic order in devastated Kosovo, where the Serbs live in constant fear of extermination.

The example of Kosovo and Metohija shows that the U.S. and the West have a double standard when it comes to terrorists. I know I have no time, but please look at the *Washington Post* of August 26, 2004, which carried a story about an Australian who was captured in Afghanistan and is being tried for war crimes. The article says that Hicks converted to Islam, joined the Kosovo Liberation Army, received training in an al Qaeda camp and took up arms against the U.S. in Afghanistan.

The question arises to illustrate this double standard: was Hicks a Taliban-al Qaeda war criminal when he was fighting against Americans in Afghanistan or was he also a Taliban-al Qaeda war criminal when he was fighting against Serbs as a member of the

KLA? Practically every day a piece of information like this one comes to light.

JUDGE PATRICK ROBINSON: Mr. Milosevic, in view of the extended break that we had to take for technical reasons, and the fact that you had to slow down, and I notice now that you are speeding up, I should tell you that the Chamber has considered that if you need it, you may have the first session tomorrow morning. Only if you need it.

PRESIDENT SLOBODAN MILOSEVIC: I certainly need it. I need much more than that, but I will certainly make use of the additional time.

Therefore, while American planes were transporting al Qaeda terrorists in chains from Afghanistan to Guantanamo, the puppet regime in Belgrade at the same time received a demand to unconditionally release all Albanian terrorists from prison. The explanation was that they were political prisoners not just plain murderers. The murderers were released. I think that the consequences of what the Clinton Administration did in support of terrorists is evident, both in the U.S. and elsewhere, and now they have become the greatest threat to the modern world. The Clinton Administration, throughout its term in office, applied this policy of double standards, which has now turned most brutally against the Americans themselves, as can be seen from what happened on September 11.

The Aggression against Yugoslavia

Five years have passed since the aggression of the NATO pact against Yugoslavia. This is not a great deal of time, but it is enough to draw reliable conclusions about the causes of that disgusting act and its severe consequences on the lives and health, material existence and cultural values of the population of the country that came under attack. It is known for a fact, and it shall be established here through documents and competent, reliable witnesses, that the aggression had been planned and was prepared over a long period of time.

The real causes of aggression were hidden behind the propaganda of the so-called humanitarian catastrophe of the Albanian population of Kosmet. The powers that be in the NATO pact proclaimed the Albanian terrorists in Kosovo and Metohija to be peaceful civilians while they accused the military and police forces of the Federal Republic of Yugoslavia of alleged crimes against innocent civilians when, in fact, they were legally fighting against terrorists. The question should be put to them: If this were the case, then what caused the deaths of a thousand soldiers and policemen? Were they killed by these peaceful unarmed civilians? Why were so many citizens killed? Was this also caused by those peaceful unarmed civilians?

Clark himself, at the time the Commander-in-Chief of the NATO pact in Europe, whom you did not allow me to cross-examine here either about the war or about his book,[31] in which he presented this information and denied these charges in a very obvious manner. He says in his book that NATO brought forces to Macedonia, ostensibly for "the pull-out of the Verification Mission," while everyone knew that the Mission had not been endangered and that the Yugoslav authorities were concerned for the safety of each and every member of the Mission, and escorted them to the border when they expressed the desire to leave. As General Naumann testified here, they left when the war and aggression against Yugoslavia became imminent. Members of the Mission were informed to withdraw in order to make the bombardment possible.

Clark, on page 168 of his book, says that when the army of Yugoslavia, in spite of all the threats of bombardment, saw the troops of the Alliance at the border, it reacted by strengthening its forces toward the border. As that happened, Clark called General Ojdanic — that's on page 168 of his book — and asked him "Why are you continuing to bring your Army forward into Kosovo?" Ojdanic replied that this was a response to the new NATO troops in Macedonia.

And then Clark said, "From the Serbs' perspective, the buildup of his forces made perfect sense. But it is also a pretext for building up forces against the Albanians too." Therefore, when a direct threat causes the strengthening of our forces, Clark then transforms the consequence into a cause for new escalation. He reported this to Madeleine Albright — this is on page 172 of his book — that there was continuous deployment and strengthening of Serbian troops.

He is talking about an attack — not in the past tense or present progressive tense, but as something that is to be expected as a consequence of an attack. If we start with air strikes, will the Serbs attack? He says that they most certainly will attack.

Albright: "So what should we do, how can we prevent their striking the civilians?"

Clark: "We can't. Despite of our best efforts, the civilians are going to be targeted by the Serbs. It will be a race, our air strikes and the damage we cause against them, against what they can do on the ground. In the short-term they can win the race."

Albright: "So what should we do?"

Clark: "We will have to strengthen our capabilities. Ultimately, we can bring more to bear against them. We can overmatch anything they have, but it's not going to be pleasant."

That is what it says in his book. Of course, he does not mention the KLA, as can be clearly seen. He refers to battles with the KLA as attacks on civilians. But, without a doubt, the bombardment will happen, consciously planned heavy bombardment of the whole of Yugoslavia, and for a fairly long time. Therefore, he himself, at the time the Supreme Commander of NATO in Europe, discarded the main thesis that the bombardment was a response to the Serbian persecution of Albanians. Because, he says, the attacks will occur "when we start with strikes." He is also proving that Rambouillet was not any kind of unsuccessful negotiating situation, but a process planned to produce an ultimatum as the basis for moving from peace to war. In fact, he is proving that the unscrupulous bombardment of towns, villages, infrastructure and the enormous human casualties were not a mistake but a calculated race — pouring fuel onto the flames from a safe distance in order to burn down whatever could be burned down as soon as possible, and then the fire-fighter, whose duty it is in all fire conditions to spare human casualties and to prevent theft and crimes, will be responsible.

Clark admits that he personally planned the air operation against Yugoslavia. He wanted the crisis in Kosovo to develop in a way so that he would be able to introduce the NATO variant. I expect that Wesley Clark will be issued a summons to come here and testify, and then we will see whether you will consider at all charging him for the crimes he committed in the former Yugoslavia, for which you claim to have the jurisdiction, or whether you will fail to do that as well. Then I will provide reliable and authoritative evidence that will unmistakably confirm the assertion that the NATO pact — or, I should not say the NATO pact, I should rather say the Clinton Administration, since Clark was one of its closest associates — has falsified the reasons for their aggression against the Federal Republic of Yugoslavia.

Canadian General Lewis Mackenzie, one of the former commanders of UNPROFOR in Bosnia, says in his text published in the

Canadian daily, *The National Post*, on April 6, 2004, that: "NATO sprung into action and, in spite of the fact no member nation of the alliance was threatened, commenced bombing not only Kosovo, but the infrastructure and population of Serbia itself — without the authorizating United Nations resolution.... Those of us who warned that the West was being sucked in on the side of an extremist, militant Kosovo-Albanian movement were dismissed as appeasers. The fact that the lead organization spearheading the fight for independence, the Kosovo Liberation Army (KLA), was universally designated a terrorist organization and known to be receiving support from Osama bin Laden's al-Qaeda, was conveniently ignored." And we will present relevant documents.

Mackenzie continues and, contrary to what this illegal Prosecution insists on in their groundless indictment, he says: "All the information that served as a cover to justify the bombing of Serbia turned out to be serious forgeries."

General Lewis Mackenzie is no pro-Serb Canadian — he is merely a professional soldier. Speaking about the campaign to expel from Kosovo all non-Albanians so that Kosovo could link up with mother Albania and fulfill the objective of a Greater Albania, Mackenzie says: "The campaign started with their attacks on Serbian security forces in the early 1990s and they were successful in turning Milosevic's heavy-handed response into worldwide sympathy for their cause. There was no genocide as claimed by the West — the 100,000 allegedly buried in mass graves turned out to be around 2,000, of all ethnic origins, including those killed in combat during the war itself."

Let us not even speak about how many of those were killed by the KLA. You have here in prison this Limaj, who is charged with the murder of nine Serbs and thirteen Albanians. Well, he only had nine Serbs in the prison, so he killed them all, but out of a larger number of Albanians he had in prison, he picked thirteen to kill. We have witnesses who will tell you and the international public how many Albanians were killed and how by the KLA, and all this was ascribed to the Serbs. Instead, you are playing with these numbers with your so-called experts, who are performing statistical calculations about the possible number of victims. This is senseless in any kind of judicial process that pretends to be a criminal procedure.

Mackenzie goes on to say: "The Kosovo Albanians have played us like Stradivarius. We have subsidized and indirectly supported their violent campaign for an ethnically pure and independent Kosovo. We have never blamed them for being the perpetrators of the violence in the early 90s and we continue to portray them as the designated victims today in spite of evidence to the contrary. When they achieve independence with the help of our tax dollars combined with those bin Laden and al-Qaeda, just consider the message of encouragement this sends to other terrorist-supported independence movements around the world."

Mackenzie does not mention the many other dollars received by the KLA, but we will have the opportunity to present this as well. He goes on: "Since the NATO/UN intervention in 1999, Kosovo has become the crime capital of Europe. The sex slave trade is flourishing. The province has become an invaluable transit point for drugs en route to Europe and North America. Ironically, the majority of the drugs came from another state 'liberated' by the West, Afghanistan. Members of the demobilized, but not eliminated, KLA are intimately involved in organized crime and the government."

Admiral Gregory Johnson, the commander of NATO forces in Kosovo, that is, the commander of the NATO Southern Force, stated in Kosovo on the occasion of the crimes committed in March 2004 that the conflicts which unfolded constituted an action of ethnic cleansing that was orchestrated in advance by Kosovo Albanians. It was an action of ethnic cleansing orchestrated in advance!

Damjan de Krnjevic-Miskovic, an editor of the U.S. magazine *National Interest* and an associate of the Center for South-Eastern Studies, in an article published in *The Wall Street Journal* under the title "Kristallnacht in Kosovo," emphasized that the Serbs had issued warnings about the true nature of the Albanian movement for years and that the West claimed that they were making this up and exaggerating. Krnjevic characterizes this anti-Serb activity and the position of the Serbian people in Kosmet in the following way: "Murder upon murder, kidnapping upon kidnapping, arson upon arson, and now finally this pogrom, have led the Serbs to the realization that they are at the mercy of barbarians." I would like to add that all this was under the auspices of the United Nations.

In his article "Kristallnacht in Kosovo," he reports that 3,000 people have been kidnapped and killed since June 1999. This is what I already told you, and that is, the mission of the United Nations in Kosovo "has been deceiving the world for the past five years with their alleged successes when in fact they were enabling militarization."

Like General Mackenzie, Krnjevic also quotes Derek Chapel, the spokesman of the NATO police, who stated, "It was planned in advance," and then, based on that, concluded, and I quote: "All that was needed was a pretext. It is clear that some in the Kosovo Albanian leadership believe that by cleansing all remaining Serbs from the area (having already achieved the cleansing of two-thirds of Kosovo's Serbs after ... 1999) ... they can present the international community with a *fait accompli*. But ethnic purity cannot be allowed to be the foundation for ... independence."

The Florida Times-Union Daily, shortly before the March 1999 escalations of Albanian terrorism in Kosovo, therefore prior to the escalation in 2004, recommended that Kosovo be returned to Serbia, and I quote: "It is finally time that Kosmet be returned to its true owners."

Ruins and Devastation

Reporters from the Russian news agency *Novosti* informed their readership about the scale of the Albanian extremist activities in an article entitled "Vandals of the 21st Century." *Novosti* reported that the aggressively minded segment of the Albanian population was destroying Christian holy places, I quote, "probably because these Christian holy places are direct evidence of the life and existence of Serbs in the territory of Kosovo from ancient times and because these holy places represent an authentic history which cannot be negated or eradicated from collective memory." The conduct of the protectorate power toward the outrages committed by the Albanian terrorists in Kosmet are characterized in the following fashion: "Each time there are new crimes against Serbs, the leaders of the protectorate raise their voices and express condolences — the condolences of accomplices."

So it is those who are in power and command responsibility there [in Kosovo], and use all of those attributes to the greatest possible degree here [in The Hague]. And they have four times the number of forces that we had at the time when it was possible to maintain public order and peace and protect the citizenry in all of the territory of Kosovo. Prominent Russian historian Natalia Norshchinskaya, who is also the deputy president of the Committee for International Relations of the State Duma of Russia, in a text entitled "Kosovo, the Monstrous Boil on the Body of Europe," which was published in Belgrade in the Serbian newspaper *Ogledalo* on July 14, 2004, says that these are, and I quote, "the bitter fruits of anti-Serbian phobia in the West." The author further stresses that it has still not been discussed and that, I quote: "practically not a single crime ascribed to the Serbian army and police has been proven with evidence" and that The Hague Tribunal, "established in order to justify aggression against the sovereign Federal Republic of Yugoslavia, has been a complete fiasco."

The well-known and respectable London *Financial Times*, addressing the dilemma of whether Kosovo will ever be safe, answers by pointing out that this first of all depends on, and I quote, "whether the West will reconsider and review its policy towards Kosovo from the very beginning. The news from Kosmet indicates that members of KFOR not only regard the Albanians favorably, but permit the outrages of the Albanian terrorists to take place." It reported that a KFOR soldier prevented a Serb from putting out the fire in his own house by saying, "Tonight everything Serbian must burn."

German members of KFOR looked on quietly as terrorists burned down four churches, demolished the monastery of Saint Archangels and desecrated the grave and monument of Emperor Dusan. After all, this was not the first time that they did something like that, to burn a Serbian seminary, set fire to a thirty-year-old disabled Serbian woman, burn the statue of the Holy Mother of Ljeviska in the church named after her and the fresco of the philosopher Plato that was inside.

A German officer coldly and cynically commented on the burning and destruction of medieval Orthodox churches of enormous cultural and national significance in Prizren and its environs by saying, "Well, those churches are very old anyway."

I will skip over the propaganda activities and the statements of various figures from the West. I will mention only Kinkel, who on May 27, 1992, said that "the Serbs should be brought to their knees." Helmut Kohl in 1993 said, "Let the Serbs drown in their own stench." Blair in 1999 said that war against Serbia was no longer a military conflict but a battle between good and evil, between civilization and barbarism. I would also add that Clinton said on April 23 and 25, 1999: "The Serbs are inflicting terror and raping Albanian children."

It was in such political, psychological and — I will take the liberty of saying — such a psychopathological situation that the NATO pact aggression against Yugoslavia was carried out. This has already been documented here. I have shown a large number of photographs of the bombardment, but this is also part of the voluminous documentation that I will submit as evidence with my opening statement. Apparently, it was not enough for the planners of NATO crimes that they destroyed and damaged so many Yugoslav and Serbian facilities and killed and wounded many Yugoslav citizens. They even bombed the Chinese Embassy, killed some Chinese and destroyed their embassy. The use of ammunition with depleted uranium polluted the ground and this contamination will remain for thousands of years.

It can be said with certainty that the pollution of the environment is not simply confined to the territory of Yugoslavia, but this pollution affects a broader area of Eastern Europe. Ammunition with depleted uranium was used most extensively in Kosovo and Metohija. This is an area of many river springs that flow into the West and South Morava Rivers, so it is obvious that the intent was to poison the Velika Morava, Sava and Danube Rivers, practically all of Serbia's waters. NATO has purposely caused an ecological catastrophe by contaminating major rivers as well as springs of mineral and medicinal waters and one must bear in mind that Serbia is one of the richest areas in Europe with respect to such mineral springs.

Yugoslavia thought it had a future in producing food for Western Europe and America, because until the NATO aggression, we had unpolluted soil and clean waters. We were producing much sought-after organically grown food and had long-term plans for agriculture up to the year 2020 in Yugoslavia, where biologically or organically grown food had special preference. Such production has been damaged for a long time to come after 78 days of bombardment, when many impermissible chemicals were used. According to the findings and opinions of experts in the District Court in Belgrade in connection with the indictment against NATO leaders, cluster bombs were dropped from aircraft, and scattered widely over large areas. This is why it is not possible to evaluate their effect strictly on military targets, even though their use against military targets is a crime, but they struck civilians and civilian targets over a much broader area. One part....

JUDGE PATRICK ROBINSON: Mr. Milosevic, I am sorry to interrupt but I think we have to leave it here for the day. We will adjourn now and resume tomorrow morning at 9:00.

Whereupon the hearing was adjourned at 2:00 p.m., to be reconvened on Wednesday, September 1, 2004, at 9:00 a.m.

THE SECOND DAY — WEDNESDAY, SEPTEMBER 1, 2004

[Defense Opening Statement]

[Open Session]

—— Upon commencing at 9:05 a.m.

JUDGE PATRICK ROBINSON: Mr. Milosevic, the concluding part of your opening statement.

PRESIDENT SLOBODAN MILOSEVIC: Mr. Robinson, I hope you will bear in mind that we began after a delay.

During the NATO aggression, toxic weapons were not used directly, but, all the same, the consequences they caused were similar to those of chemical warfare, only in a different way. As, for example, by bombing plants and warehouses containing chemicals, oil refineries and chemical factories in Pancevo, Novi Sad, Lucani and Baric. In this fashion, chemical warfare was waged against Serbia.

This was done by the powers that be, which do not like the sovereignty of Serbia in Kosovo and Metohija, although it is guaranteed by the conditions of the cease-fire and contained in Resolution 1244, which is not being respected at all. Their interest is to use the territory of Kosmet for their own geostrategic and economic goals of exploiting mineral wealth, water and other natural resources in Kosovo. We should also bear in mind that Kosovo contains the largest lignite deposits in Europe, with close to 14 billion tons. Forty-eight percent of all reserves of lead and zinc ores in Serbia are located in Kosovo, and their value is enormous. Kosmet also has large reserves of cobalt and nickel, which are also very valuable. And the electricity generating plants are very important for meeting Serbia's energy needs.

All this bespeaks the plunderous motivation of the so-called Western warriors for the human rights of Kosovo Albanians. It is evident that the source of the overall crisis in Kosovo and Metohija, which has been going on ever since the Turkish occupation of that area and the persecution of the Serbian and other non-Albanian population to this very day, is the Albanian nationalists' desire to create a Greater Albania. They do not conceal this aspiration and they shun no means of achieving that goal. This so-called Prosecution is impudent enough to include in its indictment against me and the Serbs that we wanted to create a so-called Greater Serbia in the middle of the state of Serbia, on territory that is the very heart of the medieval Serbian state.

How Serbia, whether great or small, can be created in Serbia itself is something that they themselves are unable to explain or prove. And this is best demonstrated by the first part of this operation that you call a trial, which, like the remainder of that operation, thanks to the nature and contents of this false indictment, is assuming the appearance and character of an ordinary farce.

The content and level of the farce is cheap, but not the money allocated for it, for example, by Saudi Arabia, the U.S., George Soros and other ostensibly impartial donors.

Let me also add that in 1998, when Holbrooke visited us in Belgrade, we pointed out to the USA, based on the information we had at our disposal, that the KLA is being aided by Osama bin Laden, who was in Northern Albania. He was arming, training and preparing the members of that terrorist organization in Albania; however, the Americans decided to cooperate with the KLA, and thereby, directly cooperate with bin Laden, despite the fact that he had earlier bombed U.S. embassies in Kenya and in Tanzania, and had already declared war against them.

I am convinced that one day this will have to come to light, this link, and that the time will soon come when Clinton, Albright and others will have to be held accountable, if not for what happened to the Serbs, then at least for what happened to their own people.

I will read one more quotation and then I will have to move onto other topics. "The air strikes and state coups unprecedented in their magnitude, terror and acts of sabotage, assassinations, murders of leading statesmen, superiority and attacks against all enemy lines of defense that will occur at the stroke of a single second irrespective of losses — this is the war of the future."

I assume this reminds you of what the NATO forces did to Yugoslavia in 1999 in the course of an aggression, which this side is obliged to examine but refuses to do so. But this quotation does not belong to Clinton or to Clark, although it fully describes what they did. The quotation is Hitler's. This was published in *The New York Times* in 1940 from the book *My Confidential Conversations with Hitler* by Herman Rauschning. In this book, [Hitler] further states that: "No so-called international law, and no treaties will prevent me from seizing the opportunity that presents itself." And then he goes on to speak about how he will invade France, how he will enter France as liberator, and how he will convince the middle class that he has come in order to establish the rule of law and social order, above all, a just social order.

Croatian Separatism

With regard to the war in Slovenia and Croatia, to begin with I will only mention briefly that in Warren Zimmermann's book[32] — he was the last U.S. ambassador to the SFRY — on page 173, he makes the following comment on the position of the JNA and the so-called heroic struggle in Slovenia and Croatia against the still legal Yugoslav army: "The JNA was in its own country. Its troops were, quite normally, stationed in camps in every Yugoslav Republic. After Slovenia and Croatia declared independence, however, these troops were seen as occupiers, even if they never stirred from their garrisons." The Slovenian tactics and later on — very well, I will slow down — the Slovenian and then the Croatian tactics, which cannot boast of any particular heroism, were based on avoiding open conflict and by attempting to reduce the soldiers stationed in the barracks to a state of starvation, thus forcing them to leave.

"The JNA's role — one day a defender and the next day an occupier — had a wrenching ... effect on people caught in between." Further, Zimmermann, bearing in mind all the circumstances, concludes in his book that it is wrong to speak of any attack whatsoever by the JNA on Slovenia or later on Croatia.

One of the most eminent anti-Serb activists, Warren Zimmermann, who was present there, is pointing out a well-known fact that it is wrong to speak of an attack by the JNA on Slovenia and Croatia, while you here have been given the task of saying that the aggression was prepared by the JNA in its own country. The Croatian separatist tendencies in Yugoslavia did not fully disappear with the defeat and disappearance of the quisling Independent State of Croatia in World War II.

These tendencies began to be displayed quite openly in the early 1970s with the so-called Maspok movement in Croatia, which was led by a part of the leadership of the Republic. Then demands were made for the independence of Croatia, and very strong pressures as well as threats were directed against the Serbian people, even though Croats were among the most prominent state leaders who had been appointed to important positions, and they predominated in post-war Yugoslavia. Even so, a thesis about so-called Serb hegemony was constantly being fabricated in Croatia and elsewhere. We shall see later on what Serbian domination and hegemony looked like.

It is well known that until his death in 1980, Tito, who was Croat, was the absolute leader of Yugoslavia over the course of its existence from World War II. During the existence of socialist Yugoslavia, from 1945 to 1992, over a period of 47 years, Croats had been at the head of the Yugoslav government for 30 years, and during the remaining 17 years, it was all the others. Only one of them was a Serb, from 1963 to 1967, and that was Petar Stambolic. Bearing all this in mind, how can we say that it was the Serbs who dominated the country's political leadership? As for the army, your own witness described the composition of the top leadership at the time of the break-up of Yugoslavia. There was one Yugoslav, the Minister of Defense, Veljko Kadijevic, from Croatia, who came from a mixed marriage between a Serbian man and a Croatian woman; two Serbs, one from Serbia, one from Bosnia; eight Croats, two Slovenes, two Macedonians, and one Muslim.

We should add that Tito's closest collaborator, who was the creator of the constitutional system at all levels, was a Slovene, Edvard Kardelj. All this shows quite clearly that the story of some kind of Serbian domination in Yugoslavia is a lie, pure and simple, as is the statement that the Croats and Slovenes had cause to complain of inequality and insufficient representation. The story of Serb hegemony was merely a propaganda tool which was directed against the truth, and which was used to justify secessionist aspirations.

The Ustasha genocide against the Serbs was a topic that was not discussed very often in post-war Yugoslavia. The remaining Serbs in the territory of the former Independent State of Croatia, especially those in the Krajina, which the well-known Serbian poet Matija Beckovic described as the remnants of a slaughtered people, tacitly agreed not to talk about the sufferings of their relatives, and they even acquiesced not to bury them properly. The mass graves in Jadovno, Pribilovci, and Golubnjaca were simply paved over with concrete and consigned oblivion, but the story being spread here was that the Serbs had reburied their dead later on, even though these people had never been given a proper burial. What could the Serbs in Croatia have felt, bearing in mind the terrible mass crimes from the not so distant past, when in February 1990 at an HDZ rally in Zagreb, the president of that Party, Tudjman, said, among other things, that the Independent State of Croatia was not simply a quisling creation and fascist crime, it was also an expression of the historic aspirations of the Croatian people. It was natural for them to raise their voices before "the Croatian people," in quotation marks because this was not referring to all Croats, but to extremists who were receiving aid from abroad, before they set out once again to realize their so-called historic aspirations. You have all this information and you are disregarding it.

This illegal indictment did not refrain from discussing in paragraph 94 illegal indictments against the HDZ without any qualifications, even though this was the party that revived the practices and symbols from the Ustasha era. At the same time the pro-Yugoslav Serbian Democratic Party was referred to as a nationalist party in paragraph 95 of this same false indictment. They permit themselves such a manipulation in this kind of presentation because they know all about the chauvinist activities of the HDZ, but they are not going to allow a single word to be said about it. Everything about the HDZ has to be suppressed, and the SDS has to be blackened. This very clearly shows that the activities of the Serbian people — what they fail to say is that the activities of the Serbian people were carried out in self-defense.

Warren Zimmermann, in his book *Origins of a Catastrophe*, discusses how in Tudjman's Croatia, and I quote, "He presided over serious violations of the rights of Serbs. They were dismissed from work, required to take loyalty oaths." The irony is all the greater here because they tried to impute that I requested some kind of statements of loyalty. Well, they could not find a single person who had signed any statement of loyalty to me. This is absurd.

Their homes and property were attacked, Zimmermann continues, and says that Tudjman's ministers referred to Serbs by derogatory names. Zimmermann did not join them, but he did not stop them, either. On page 215 of his book, he says that Tudjman played a major role both in the violent death of Yugoslavia and in the war in Croatia and in Bosnia-Herzegovina. He emphasized Tudjman's racist attitude toward the Serbs on account of which, he claimed, Croatia had turned into an undemocratic and explosive republic. Those are his words.

The anti-Serbian path the new Croatian government has taken is linked to the Nerval Group. Nerval is a place in Canada where there is a large concentration of pro-Ustasha Franciscan monks from Herzegovina. The Canadian Ministry of Foreign Affairs assessed that these neo-Ustasha organizations in Canada were more extreme than the actual pro-Nazi Ustasha organization in Hitler's Independent State of Croatia. The Croatian press writes freely about this now. Due to the shortage of time, I cannot present this to you now, but the gist of it is that, as early as 1987, the first step had been taken toward the future Independent State of Croatia, a program containing four main points, which I took from the Croatian magazine *Globus*. First, Croatia must be an independent state at any cost. Second, we must work on making Croatia an ethnically pure and homogeneous state. In other words, the Serb national community should be reduced to a negligible minority so it can no longer be a disruptive factor.

Third, the struggle in Croatia should be led on one front, and the main adversaries are the Serbs. In order to defeat the Serbs, we need to join together with the Communists and the Partisans, and we will win our final victory in a firm alliance with them. And four: As far as Bosnia-Herzegovina is concerned, such a policy should be conducted that will sooner or later lead to the unification of Western Herzegovina, a pure Croatian territory, with Croatia. Martin Spegelj, Tudjman's defense minister at the time these events were taking place, said publicly in *Dnevnik* on October 28, 2001, that: "If a house belonging to a Serb is burned down, he will not have a place to return to." He explained that Gojko Susak had said precisely this. Again in Novi Sad on October 29, 2001, Martin Spegelj revealed that Tudjman and Susak drew the essential concept of a pure nation state by using the World War II Independent State of Croatia as a model. On December 8, 1993, *The New York Times* discussed the 10,000 homes that had been dynamited. I am not going to quote any further from that in order to save time.

The Serbian people in Croatia, besides suffering the pressure, harassment, physical attacks, and overall degradation on an individual as well as collective level, were also exposed to collective legal discrimination. The Christmas Constitution is well known. It deprived the Serbs of their status as a constituent people, which they had enjoyed under all prior Croatian constitutions. In his *Balkan Odyssey*, Lord Owen says on page 61, that the Serbs resisted in a fashion similar to the resistance they gave to the incorporation into Croatia of territories settled by Serbs in Northern Dalmatia, Lika, Banija, Slavonia and Baranja, territories forming the Military Border or Krajina between the Habsburg Empire, which had been ruled by Vienna and not by Zagreb, and the Ottoman Empire. This resistance was especially strong after 1945 because this population had been subjected to genocide by the Croatian Ustashas during World War II.

In 1995, very few commentators realized or recognized that the Croatian government, in attacking Krajina, was not liberating this land since the Serbs had inhabited it for over three centuries. This is what Lord Owen writes.

Already by the mid-1990s, there was a series of attacks and killings because the Serbs reacted by placing barricades on the roads approaching their settlements, which is why this revolt was called the "log revolution." The Croatian authorities treated this reaction by the Serbs, who were afraid of finding themselves without any means for collective defense against the newly recurring Ustasha ideology and terror, as an attack constituting aggression against the Croatian state. It is hard to explain how one can attack a state by placing logs on the roads leading to private homes.

Spegelj said: "In Knin, our solution will be to massacre them. For that, we have international recognition." There are numerous proofs that this is how it happened. These are not empty words; we are talking about dead people.

Gregory Elich writes in his book, *The Invasion of Serbian Krajina*, of what Tudjman said in 1990: "I am glad that my wife in neither a Serb nor a Jew." He also reminds us that Tudjman maintained that accounts of the Holocaust were exaggerated and one-sided.

I will cite just a few of the many quotes from Elich's book: "During its violent secession from Yugoslavia in 1991, Croatia expelled more than 300,000 Serbs, and Serbs were eliminated from ten towns and 183 villages. Tomislav Mercep, until recently the advisor to the minister of the Internal Affairs of Croatia and a member of Parliament, was the leader of a death squad that murdered 2,500 Serbs in Western Slavonia in 1991 and 1992. In Croatia, they speak about this as 'heroic deeds.'"

You have here a testimony of Miro Bajramovic, a member of that death squad. I have it on tape, but I do not have time to play it for you.

Gregory Elich goes on to say that the Clinton Administration extended recognition to Croatia because it corresponded to its geopolitical interests.

Susan Woodward says in her book, *Balkan Tragedy*: "The Croatian government ... did little to protect its citizens from vicious outbursts of anti-Serb terror in some mixed communities in Dalmatia and in the interior in the summer months of 1989, when Croat zealots smashed store-fronts, fire-bombed homes, and harassed or arrested potential Serbian leaders.... Serbs were expelled from jobs because of their nationality."

All this was happening in 1989, while you are ascribing a "joint criminal enterprise" to the Serbs when they were in fact defending themselves. Chris Hedges, in *The New York Times* of June 16, 1997, writes that 500,000 out of 600,000 ethnic Serbs were cleansed from the country by Tudjman. He talks about *Kristallnacht* in Zadar, and expulsion of tens of thousands of people from their apartments.

You can find other articles in the Croat papers, *Feral* and *Tjednik* about the crimes that took place in Vukovar, as early as 1990 before the fighting started. I am quoting from them that corpses of dead Serbs were floating down the Danube, and that crimes were committed in Gospic and on the Croatian seacoast.

A Croatian magazine, *Identitet*, reported that very little had been done to shed light on the crimes committed in Osijek in 1991 and 1992, when several dozen Serbian civilians were killed, and it then went on to describe how they were taken away and how they were killed.

On the subject of Gospic, three officers from the Croatian army arrived here to testify about those crimes. But they were not given any protection, so Milan Levar, a witness who was supposed to testify against those who committed the Gospic massacre, was liquidated. You provided protection for [Drazen] Erdemovic, who admitted that he had killed 100 people in Srebrenica, and whom we had arrested. He came here because he asked to be brought to The Hague. We extradited him at his own request because he was not our citizen.

Even though Erdemovic admitted to killing 100 people, you released him after four years so he can live unpunished, but you did not protect the witnesses from Gospic. I see that I will have to skip some things. Time flies, unfortunately.

David Owen, on page 182 of his book, writes that the Serbs who remained in the JNA did not have any freedom at all. Many JNA barracks had been surrounded and blockaded by the Croatian army, which was one of the reasons why the JNA reacted so forcefully in places like Vukovar. He says that Vukovar was the only place where the JNA reacted so forcefully. But he does explain why this happened. The explanation is also now being written up in the Croatian press, about how many Serbian corpses were floating down the Danube long before anything happened in Vukovar. Vukovar is an exception, and it is the only place where the JNA responded so forcefully, to use Owen's words, to the encirclement of its soldiers, and to attacks against them as well as against the civilian population.

Therefore, there is no doubt that the war in Croatia was incited and initiated by the Croatian authorities. The objective was violent and illegal secession and, as it will be shown later, the achievement of an ethnically pure Croatian state. That is why the Serbs were forced to defend themselves. They had to fight for their survival. Therefore, nobody doubts the existence of individual crimes, which resulted from the ensuing chaos, but this so-called indictment is trying to present them as the result of some kind of joint criminal undertaking, although all the historical, legal and military facts speak to the contrary.

You base the indictment on such testimonies as the one given by Milan Babic and the testimonies of similar witnesses. But Babic was in conflict with his own leadership precisely because of his own extremism.

It is well known that the Vance Plan[33] was adopted, primarily thanks to the efforts of Cyrus Vance himself, but also thanks to the efforts of the Republic of Serbia as well as my own efforts.

Protected zones were created, but the Croatian army never respected them. It is well known how many attacks were launched against them: the Miljevacki Plateau, Perucica, Medak Pocket, Zemunik, Western Slavonia, operations Flash and Storm, and so on. It is also well known how many hundreds of Serbs were killed in each one of those attacks and all that happened.

Weapons were kept under lock and key. The Serbs took them in order to defend their own lives and prevent a massacre. Lord Owen, who discusses all this in his book, says: "The Croatian army equipped itself quickly with planes and heavy artillery. All of this came from neighboring European countries and was bought in the former East Germany. When this happened, it was not difficult to see why the Serbs resisted demilitarization and demobilization. The Serb factor was a consolidating factor, and the Croatian side was a destabilizing factor."

Owen also states that the greatest ethnic cleansing in the Yugoslav crisis was the one before which this institution remains indifferent. He is talking about the expulsion of thousands of Serbs from Croatia and the killing of hundreds. When something like that happens to Serbs, it does not appear to be crime.

The Muslims in Bosnia

I will say a few words about Bosnia-Herzegovina. It is well known that peace lasted there as long as Yugoslavia lasted, with a brief time lag.

The absence of tutors and occupiers had oriented the citizens of this multi-cultural society toward one another. In Article 1 of the amended Constitution of July 31, 1991, the drafter wrote that Bosnia-Herzegovina is a democratic, sovereign state and an equal community of all of its citizens — Muslims, Serbs, Croats and members of other nationalities who live there. That Socialist Republic of Bosnia-Herzegovina was also an integral part of Yugoslavia.

This was written in the amended constitution. However, even though this peaceful life of the population in this republic continued to last, you can still see now on the website of the Bosnian organization *Young Muslims*, which was founded in 1939, an oath which they created in the second half of 1947 in which they discuss an uncompromising struggle against everything that is not Islamic, and that they will give all for the divine, that they will sacrifice everything, including their own lives, if this is in the interest of Islam. How can one wage an uncompromising battle in a multi-ethnic community like Bosnia and Yugoslavia against everything that is not Islamic, especially considering that when the above-cited oath was created a great majority of the population of Bosnia-Herzegovina was non-Islamic?

And it so happened that these same Young Muslims and their like-minded associates had found a way open to them for the realization of their goal and found the means placed in their hands to conduct a holy war.

The first national political party that was created was Izetbegovic's Party of Democratic Action [SDA]. It is characteristic that the founder of the party and Izetbegovic's sponsor, Izet Adil Zulfikarpasic speaks about the first party meeting in Novi Pazar, a city in Serbia, in his book and says: "When we came to Novi Pazar, we were welcomed by a great mass of people. The authorities were quite fair, and the police too. Patrol cars made sure that everything took place without incident. When we arrived in the town itself, the police officers withdrew from the streets and we could see only SDA guards everywhere. But then something happened at this rally that surprised me considerably. The meeting was organized in a pro-fascist way. There were hundreds of religious flags waving in the stadium."

And Zulfikarpasic goes on to say in his book: "Large numbers of imams would appear all at once wherever we went. They were our hosts and they had organized everything. Religious officials joined the party. At some point, I requested that the flags be removed.

Then people began to appear dressed in caftans and *dzelabija*, which nobody had ever worn in Bosnia on any occasion."

I will omit that Zulfikarpasic left the party because he did not want any part in it. Anyway, it is well-known that Izetbegovic, as far back as the spring of 1943, had led the Muslim youth in Sarajevo, and in that capacity he hosted Amin al-Husseini, the Grand Mufti of Jerusalem, Hitler's friend who fled to Germany. Al-Husseini advocated *jihad*, a holy war against Christians and Jews. A Muslim Waffen SS Division was established during Pavelic's Independent State of Croatia on the initiative of [Heinrich] Himmler[34] and through the mediation of this same Husseini. And there were more. A Handzar Division, a Kama Division, and also a Skenderbeg Division of Muslims from Kosovo and Metohija and from Western Macedonia were formed.

Unfortunately, I have to move through this very quickly. In 1990 Izetbegovic republished his *Islamic Declaration*, in which he talks about "the creation of a single Islamic Community from Morocco to Indonesia" and "the incompatibility of Islamic and non-Islamic institutions" and predicts "the Islamic rebirth." He does not talk about the "rebirth" as an era of security but "as an era of unrest and temptation since there are so many things that cry out for their destroyers, and people who are asleep can be awakened only by blows."

First of all, Izetbegovic wrote that we have to be preachers and only then soldiers. The Islamic movement, according to him, can and will assume power as soon as it gains adequate moral and numerical strength to not only destroy the existing non-Islamic government but to build an Islamic government. Izetbegovic believed that members of the Islamic faith should learn, using the example of Pakistan, what should be done and what should not be done. Under the present circumstances, he said, the aspiration of all Muslims and Islamic communities in the world is the struggle for the establishment of a great Islamic federation from Morocco to Indonesia, from the tropics of Africa to Asia.

So you can imagine how Serbs and Croats, who together constituted the majority in Bosnia-Herzegovina, would have felt about such assertions, that they were supposed to live in some kind of European Pakistan. You can imagine what their reaction would have been.

However, no one can give better testimony than Islamic fundamentalists themselves on behalf of Izetbegovic's loyalty to the

Islamic fundamentalist cause. According to a Reuters report from Dubai, dated April 11, 1993, Alija Izetbegovic solemnly received an Islamic award in Riyadh, and I quote, "for his contribution to jihad, the holy war against non-believers."

This reward confirmed that Izetbegovic had persevered along the road that he had chosen as a young man, in accordance with the oath of allegiance to Young Muslims that he took in 1947, which means an uncompromising struggle against everything non-Islamic. But it was not only the Islamic fundamentalist circles that knew the nature of the Islamic regime in Bosnia-Herzegovina.

That is also clearly stated in a report of the Republican Committee [on Terrorism and Unconventional Warfare] to the U.S. Senate, dated January 16, 1997. I will go through it very quickly and will skip some parts. The second point reports that members of the military Islamic network, together with armed Iranian Revolutionary Guards and other operatives, entered Bosnia in large numbers along with thousands of Mujahedins, holy warriors from throughout the Muslim world, from the following Islamic countries: Burnei, Malaysia, Pakistan, Saudi Arabia, Sudan and Turkey. They were joined by a number of radical Muslim organizations. The role played by one allegedly humanitarian organization from Sudan is well documented.

In point number 3, the radical Islamic character of the Sarajevo regime is illustrated by profiles of its most important officials, including President Izetbegovic himself. The progressive Islamization of the Bosnian Army would include the creation of local Bosnian Mujahedin units. Credible claims are set forth that major atrocities against civilians in Sarajevo occurred and were staged for propaganda purposes by operatives of the Izetbegovic government.

Conflicts with enemies, both Muslim and non-Muslim, are described. The report states there is corroboration that [Muslims] themselves staged attacks against their own citizens. The document concludes that the American Administration's policy has given Iran an extraordinary foothold in Europe and has heedlessly endangered American lives and U.S. strategic interests.

Further, when referring to al Qaeda, it talks about the sleeper agents in Izetbegovic's government, whom you brought here as witnesses to testify against me. Also, that the Iranian [secret] service has developed those relations to such an extent that they jointly planned terrorist activities.

I am talking about all of this so that you can realize how the green light that Clinton gave led to such a degree of Iranian influence, because, as the document asserts, it involves the promotion of an Islamic revolution in Europe.

And then there is a reference to this phony humanitarian agency that is believed to be connected with Sheikh Omar Abdel-Rahman, who was convicted of the World Trade Center bombing in 1993, and to Osama bin Laden, a wealthy Saudi immigrant who is believed to be bankrolling numerous militant groups.

The same report then states that this policy allowed weapons to come to Bosnia and was of great assistance to Iran, allowing it to establish good relations with the Bosnian government. This is what a senior CIA officer told the U.S. Congress, adding that this is something that the USA will live to regret. He was more precise, stating that "when they blow up some Americans, as they no doubt will before this ... thing is over, it will be in part because the Iranians were able to have the time and contacts to establish themselves well in Bosnia."[35]

I also wish to note that today, March 31, is an official holiday in Islamic Bosnia-Herzegovina, *Patriotic League Day*, commemorating a military formation that was established on March 31, 1991 by the SDA, the party which was organized along military lines a year before the conflict broke out. Documents show that in 1992, when the first conflicts broke out, one half of the total number of Serbian victims were then killed.

Analyses by experts show that the Serbs were not at all prepared for the war, whereas the Muslims had been preparing for it for an entire year.

Owen says in his book that the picture of the Bosnian Muslims as being unarmed remained unchanged even after Alija Izetbegovic himself admitted openly on television that they were being armed through secret channels, and that the Bosnian government had obtained tens of thousands of guns, millions of bullets, tens of thousands of mines and bombs, and a hundred thousand uniforms.

According to Sefer Halilovic, the Chief of Staff of the Army of Bosnia and Herzegovina, in an interview he gave to *Nasi Dani* on September 25, 1992, when the war started — and this is 1992, gentlemen — the Patriotic League had staff members in nine regional and 103 municipal locations, as well as 98,000 fighters. They had a staff in 103 municipalities, while Bosnia-Herzegovina had a total of 109 municipalities altogether!

Everything is clear as far as war preparations are concerned. It is clear to everyone but you!

The Serbian side had three objectives. This can be seen when the entire political situation is analyzed. The first was to preserve the Yugoslav Federation, and then, if it was impossible to achieve that objective, to attain the right of their own self-determination just as the other peoples in Yugoslavia enjoyed this right. In case this objective was also unattainable, then to find ways through negotiation to ensure an equitable position for the Serbs in Bosnia-Herzegovina.

The support of the Serbian side for the preservation of Yugoslavia for me was the only position that was in line with national and international law, but reasons of fairness and practicality also worked in favor of that position. Unfortunately, there was no more time for that, while the justification for the demands of the Serbian people in Bosnia to have equal rights had deep roots because the Serbian people have inhabited Bosnia-Herzegovina for more than a millennium.

I have to speed up the chronological presentation of these events. We will have the opportunity to deal with this through witnesses, who will also indicate that the Serbian actions were reactions to what the Muslim and Croatian sides were doing in violation of the constitutional rights of the Serbs. And what the Serbs did was only in proportion to these violations, to protect the rights which the other two sides, by means of illegal actions, had taken away from them.

The Serbian side was gradually moving away from its demands until it finally reached the position that represented the minimum which the Serbs would accept so as not to jeopardize their national rights and, perhaps, even their very survival. Finally, the Dayton Accords sanctioned their rights, but unfortunately, this happened only after a great deal of unnecessary bloodshed.

It is well known that the last chance to preserve peace in Bosnia and Herzegovina before the war was the Cutileiro Plan. All three parties signed onto the Plan, but when Zimmermann urged Izetbegovic against it, Izetbegovic withdrew his signature from the Plan. I believe that we will have ample documents about this to present later. All of this goes to show very clearly that the Serbian side was not the one that wanted war and that it did its best to prevent war. This was especially true because, after international recognition and the outbreak of the war — and it is no accident that these two events coincided — the JNA began withdrawing from Bosnia-Herzegovina in accordance with the previously signed agreement. This is stated in the report of the Secretary General of the United Nations Butros-Ghali of May 30, 1992, addressed to the Security Council, which also states that the Army of the Republika Srpska, established on May 15, was not under the control of Belgrade. And it also states that a considerable part of the territory of Bosnia-Herzegovina had been occupied by the official forces of the Republic of Croatia.

However, the president of the Security Council at the time, the Austrian Peter von Fellner, withheld and concealed Boutros-Ghali's report until the Security Council voted for sanctions against the Federal Republic of Yugoslavia. The situation described in the withheld report was the basis for the imposition of sanctions on Croatia, and by no means on the Federal Republic of Yugoslavia.

These are all the facts that I have managed to present over this short period of time, and this is, I should say, only the tip of the iceberg. And what have you now put forward against these indisputable historical and material facts, against the truth?

The Real Perpetrators

In this false indictment, you have mechanically compiled an unnatural composite of events and crimes, and you branded it "joint criminal enterprise," doubtlessly without a shred of evidence for the kind of plan and the intentions that you are imputing to the Serbs!

However, the fact this so-called Prosecution relied on a unique concept called a "joint criminal enterprise" is itself proof that it cannot establish guilt. The very absence of evidence — with respect to someone's deeds as well as intentions — compel one to resort to such a nebulous construction as "joint criminal enterprise." In other words, when there is evidence of a person's offence and a person's intentions, a legal prosecution has no need to rely on a "joint criminal enterprise," but instead it uses evidence pertaining to actual deeds and intent. The use of such methods for indictments is resorted to when the prosecutor does not have evidence and cannot establish guilt and uses this method to avoid the burden of proof, which is an integral part of any legal judicial system in every indictment.

This was conceived so that innocent people could be accused without proof of guilt. And that, of course, is nothing short of a sheer mutilation of justice. What is written there is utterly empty, because in these indictments, in these so-called indictments, you speak of crimes we did not commit, intentions we never had. That is your concept.

You have no proof either for Bosnia or Croatia, where Serbia had no jurisdiction, but we did assist the Serbs. Of course we did, and we would have been the lowest scum of the earth had we not helped them when their lives were in peril. But the greatest aid we provided was to establish peace.

Of greatest assistance was also the fact that during all those ten years there was no discrimination in Serbia on ethnic grounds against anyone in any way.

On the subject of Kosovo, there is not a single shred of evidence that any crime was committed, not only under anyone's orders but also with any kind of foreknowledge on the part of the generals in command or anyone else. In spite of all this, you have indicted four generals. Not a single one of them issued any orders to that effect, nor did a single one have any knowledge about anything that could have constituted a crime before it had actually occurred.

You have accused the political leadership of Serbia and Yugoslavia, and you have all the evidence showing that those who committed individual crimes in Kosovo and Metohija, even during the crazed day and night bombardment, were apprehended by the state authorities, and that they were arrested and were brought to justice. Even your witness here, General Vasiljevic confirmed the details about a meeting that I had with the top echelons of military and state security and with the General Staff, when I personally insisted that all perpetrators of crimes must be arrested, and, as General Vasiljevic even quoted me, that there should be no exceptions. He also pointed out that the General Staff, starting with the Chairman of the Joint Chiefs of Staff, General Ojdanic, a completely innocent man who is sitting in this prison, and down to the four generals whom you have indicted without basis, Lazarevic, Pavkovic, Djordjevic, and Lukic, are in the same position. The leadership, the Supreme Command, even when considered along the vertical line, acted by means of prevention and forbade the existence of paramilitary formations.

There are written reports about this. I have submitted them as evidence, but you will get all this in several hundred reports from military courts, military prosecutors' offices, and instructions for the prosecution of criminal acts. The first reports concerned with these issues started coming at the end of March 1999, and they continue. What else could the executive government and the judiciary have done in any country other than to insist categorically on the prosecution of all perpetrators of crimes and to make sure through the reports it receives that this is being done. This is precisely what we did under the most difficult circumstances, under conditions of daily bombardment. Some trials were completed and the perpetrators convicted even during the bombardment.

You have not presented a shred of evidence to the contrary in these two years of presentation of evidence. Throughout these two years, you have not presented one single proof or a single testimony that might have indicated any link between a crime that had been committed and the troop commanders, the generals you have indicted, or the political leadership of Serbia, or me, personally. On the contrary, you have evidence that we did our utmost to prevent crimes, and if crimes were committed, and this is possible even in peacetime let alone during wartime and especially during ethnic conflicts, that perpetrators ought to be prosecuted under the law. You have the proof that the first trial for war crimes was held in Serbia, in the District Court in Sabac in 1993.

On the other hand, you have all the evidence that we were the ones who were the most persistent in achieving peace and who can claim the most credit for achieving peace, that we were the ones who saved millions of refugees on the principle of non-discrimination, because 70,000 Muslim refugees found refuge in Serbia. We freed the French pilots and other hostages, and you have proof for all of that.

You could see in intercepted communications, which you have obtained, not only that we have done everything to achieve peace, but also that we could only insist, plead and exert pressure because we did not have any other powers. But we were succeeding. Please look at these interviews because it would be enough to clear up all the matters you do not wish to understand and render your charges senseless.

On the other hand, you have a great deal of evidence showing the role of the Croatian leadership in ethnic cleansing. You have proof about the existence of such a plan and its implementation before and after 1990. You even have the shorthand reports, and we received some of these from you, from which you can see the fabrication of excuses for the perpetration of crimes during Operations Flash and Storm. You already have evidence of the role of the Clinton Administration in all this, and you will receive more evidence. You have written evidence about those who made all these decisions, because in each of the shorthand reports of the so-called VNOS, that is the Croatian Council of Defense and National Security, you can see precisely who was there.

You also have evidence of crimes against Serbs based on the decisions of the Muslim leadership. Kljujic testified here, a former member of the Presidency of Bosnia and Herzegovina, and I asked him about this. Because, on the basis of the shorthand reports of the Presidency of Bosnia and Herzegovina you can see that Izetbegovic knew about the camps where people had been illegally detained for several years. You will be able to hear more testimony about this.

You have everything you need for the [prosecution of the] Croatian and Muslim leaderships but you do not have one single thing about the leadership of Yugoslavia and Serbia. You do not have any such thing for the leadership of Republika Srpska and Republika Srpska Krajina.

You even have evidence from the testimony of your own protected witness, who was an important political leader there, that what Milan Martic said to me was correct, that in the Krajina, including Knin, the Croats who remained were being treated as equal citizens and that there was absolutely no discrimination whatsoever.

False Witnesses

A special matter which I wish to touch upon briefly is the matter of witnesses who, in accordance with your procedures, reached a plea bargain with the so-called Prosecution by admitting to a crime. And this represents, I dare say, an example of the fabrication of false witnesses. I think that in the annals of false witnesses, one stands out as unprecedented. One of these witnesses, when I asked him how he could have signed a confession that 7,000 Muslims had been shot in Srebrenica, explained that his defense had sent a letter in which it promised not to challenge any numbers. So he could have written down even 70,000! He could have written down anything he wanted.

I have already submitted documentation my collaborators were able to collect, which casts serious doubt on your construction about Srebrenica. In the meantime, we have also heard the testimony of General Morillon, who testified here that Srebrenica was a trap for [General Ratko] Mladic. Morillon confirmed, in his opinion — and he knew Mladic well — that Mladic could never have issued such an order. And this is in accordance with what I believe. I do not believe that Mladic could have issued such an order. His honor would never have allowed him to do such a dirty and dishonorable deed. But there will be an opportunity to question more witnesses about this.

It is in the interest of both Serbs and Muslims to have the truth about Srebrenica come to light rather than to create a false myth about it. Your fabrication of false witnesses and Paddy Ashdown's[36] pressure on the leadership in the Republika Srpska is not helpful in getting the truth out about Srebrenica.

Synchronized attempts are being made here and there to create a double crime, which insults both the living and the dead. Everyone should be interested in establishing the truth about Srebrenica so that those who perpetrated crimes may be punished and those who are innocent may be set free of any charges and suspicions that they committed such a dishonorable act.

You did not make use of Erdemovic to get information from him. You did not take advantage of any of the things you could have made use of to establish the truth. I hope — I can only hope, because I myself cannot provide everything — that some of the witnesses will shed more light on what happened there.

But to return to this witness or to other witnesses whom you have here on plea bargain agreements. You had the public testimony of Miroslav Deronjic; his own mother ought to refuse to speak to him in light of what he said he did and what he wrote that he did: that he slaughtered an entire village after having guaranteed its security. First he guaranteed its security, and then he slaughtered the whole village! You forgave him all of that only so that he would lie about [Radovan] Karadzic.

And you have in your hands Karadzic's order to the troops in Srebrenica that they must look after the civilians and adhere to the Geneva Convention. This was sent in writing to the troops. And then someone like Deronjic comes along to testify that Karadzic allegedly whispered in his car, so that nobody could hear it, that they should be killed. This does not make sense and it is not worth discussing. No normal man can comprehend it, especially when someone claims and signs a document about shooting 7,000 men under the obligation that such figures would not be challenged, and not because he knows it. Not to mention other matters that you made use of here.

You placed my speech in Gazimestan[37] at the foundation of your indictment. You have accused me of fanning the flames of Serbian nationalism. I am proud to this very day of that speech, because it says everything, but it certainly did not awaken any negative atmosphere. But you are not the only ones to participate in this. It has been repeated by many politicians in the West. There is hardly a newspaper that has not written about it. This lie has been used and repeated innumerable times and not in 1989 but ten years later. I have no time to dwell on this, but I am giving examples of the way manipulations and lies are perpetrated.

Ten years later, Robin Cook[38] said on June 28, 1999, that Milosevic used the important anniversary of the Battle of Kosovo, but not to give a message of hope and reform. Instead, he threatened to use force to deal with Yugoslavia's internal political difficulties. In doing so he thereby launched his personal agenda for power and spreading ethnic hatred under the cloak of nationalism.

I have here any number of quotations, all dating from 1999, 2000, 2001. Look at *The Independent* of July 1, 2001: "Serbia's leader sets out his agenda at a rally of more than a million Serbs at the Battle of Kosovo 600th anniversary celebrations, as he openly threatens force to hold the six-republic federation together."

Here you have quotations from *Time* magazine, even from the *Economist*. They are all quoting lies that were never a part of the speech. I will now quote from *The Independent* of June 29, 1989. That same paper then wrote that the Serbian president made not one aggressive reference to Albanian counter-revolutionaries. "Counterrevolution" is a definition put forward by the federal presidencies of both the party and the state in 1981. Instead of that, wrote *The Independent*, the president spoke of mutual tolerance, building of a rich and democratic society and ending the discord that he said led to Serbia's defeat here by the Turks six centuries ago.

The Independent, at the time reporting from the location, wrote: " 'There is no more appropriate place than this field of Kosovo to say that accord and harmony in Serbia are vital to the prosperity of the Serbs and all other citizens living in Serbia regardless of their nationality or religion,' he said. Mutual tolerance and cooperation were also *sine qua non* for Yugoslavia: 'Harmony and relations on the basis of equality among Yugoslavia's peoples are the precondition for its existence, for overcoming the crisis.' "

Serbian Pluralism

Therefore, when they received orders to lie, they did not even read their own newspaper's earlier reports from Gazimestan. But I do not have the time to dwell on this now.

Serbia never had an exclusively Serbian population. Today, more than ever in the past, members of other ethnic communities and religions live in it. This is not a disadvantage for Serbia. On the contrary, this is an advantage. Citizens of different nationalities and religions live together more frequently and more successfully. Therefore, all people in Serbia who live from their own labor and who are honest and respect other people and nations, are in their own Republic.

There is no point in spending my time on this. I just wanted to illustrate the extent to which the abuses go, in particular the abuses in a legal action, which pretends to be a legal procedure. Taking a few sentences out of context is considered to be immoral among intellectuals, writers, literary critics, publicists and scientists. But you not only took sentences out of context, you also took parts of sentences out of context in order to create your constructs. However, we will have time later to see all of this. In any case, it seems to me that this is not difficult to establish. I am not citing this here for any other reason than to show how unscrupulously lies are being put forth.

In Serbia, the principle of national equality enjoyed continuity during the ten years of my tenure. We have a transcript of a party conference in 1998, which was attended by 400 members of the ruling party. Kosovo, among other issues, was discussed. This was not a discussion for the benefit of the newspapers; this was a discussion of the political leadership from the ruling party, including all of its ministers, members of government, and members of the parliament.

I would like to read only an excerpt, my brief conclusion: "It is our policy to resolve the Kosovo problem by political means." I said this on June 10, 1998. Therefore, we approached that settlement having in mind our convictions and our program, which implied the principle of national equality. We did not want to inflict damage on the Albanians, nor did we want Albanians in Kosovo to be second class citizens.

And then I spoke about how many thought that perhaps the majority of Albanians were in favor of this. Bearing that in mind, I thought that perhaps the majority had been influenced by the pressure exerted on them, what was explained to them, what explanation was given to them about their future, and everything else. Then I emphasized that we have to promote a political solution and affirm the principle of national equality. We must bear in mind that those who have been manipulated were an unhappy lot and have been manipulated just like any other poor people in the world. They are manipulated first of all by their own powerful people, then by other manipulators in the world whose objective is to destabilize

Southeastern Europe, where they constantly need to have an alibi in order to keep the military forces of the great powers there. In the end, I said: Dialogue. I have emphasized that the dialogue that was started is not reserved only for the state committee and representatives of the Albanian political parties. The dialogue is not reserved solely for them and it is not solely a Serbian-Albanian dialogue, but also a Serb-Albanian-Turkish, Muslim and Roma, and Montenegrin dialogue, because the dialogue should be present at all levels because the people need to be mobilized to live.

So, these were the ten years of continuity in my commitment to a policy of national equality which preserved half of the former Yugoslavia from any conflict and war. For all those ten years. This is why I am speaking about how much this whole thing has been turned upside down. And that is why I said that this indictment represents the sum of many unscrupulous manipulations and lies, violations of the law, a defeat of morality and an extremely irresponsible revision of history.

You have embraced, with respect to the individual acts of generals, officials, or my own, the concept of command responsibility, by which you are able to convict any innocent person on the basis of such person holding a certain position. And now you are trying to bring these generals here. I have neither the time nor the possibility of speaking about these individual cases now other than to say that they have already been challenged in part in the testimonies of your own witnesses, much more in the memoirs of the participants themselves, and most of all in the numerous scholarly studies that have been written based on Western sources and documents. We will leave it up to the new witnesses, when they appear here before you, to have their say.

I would just like to point out the paradoxical situation into which you have brought yourselves by bowing to the shortsighted, merciless, day-to-day policies of the Clinton Administration.

Reality has been falsified in the name of a pragmatic political program. All three indictments were issued after nineteen NATO countries conducted an open aggression against the remaining part of Yugoslavia, against Serbia and Montenegro, with banned weapons and inflicting new forms of tyranny by means of high technology. Is there any greater cynicism?

The indictment for Croatia cites the ethnic cleansing of Croats and an alleged joint criminal enterprise which, it maintains, was conceived before August 1, 1991, and lasted until 1992. I must say that it takes extreme arrogance to put such a lie in writing. As is well known, this was a period of mass crimes against Serbs and the first major exodus of Serbs from Croatia — a hundred and fifty thousand of them.

The Kosovo indictment was issued, and I quote, "because of the expulsion of a substantial number of Albanian citizens from Kosovo." Well, you heard what Clark's book says, but you will also see many other more interesting things. You cannot cite one single village from which someone was expelled while Kosovo was under the control of the state organs of Serbia. It seems to me that you are not even paying attention to the official statements.

JUDGE PATRICK ROBINSON: Mr. Milosevic, bring your statement to an end in three minutes.

PRESIDENT SLOBODAN MILOSEVIC: Yes. I will do my best. If not in three, then in four, but it will be no longer than that. In any case, I had to skip over a lot.

You are not even monitoring official statements made by the U.S. and NATO representatives who openly state today that they needed these games with Kosovo so that NATO could extend its activities beyond the borders drawn by the agreement for the establishment of the Alliance.

The indictment for Bosnia and Herzegovina was issued for genocide, please, genocide against Muslims and Croats in Bosnia-Herzegovina. This is also extreme arrogance, when it is well known that in these evil times Belgrade was the only political center in Yugoslavia during the Yugoslav crisis from which a policy of peace was consistently conducted, the only center from which a consistent policy of national equality was conducted, and thanks to which there were no occurences of discrimination and, thanks to which throughout the entire decade of crimes, an unchanged national ethnic structure was preserved only in Serbia.

I am aware, gentlemen, that it is illusory to look for logic in a rigged trial. There have been similar cases before in history: the Dreyfus case and the Dimitrov case in connection with the burning of the Reichstag. But this trial exceeds those because of the depth of the tragic consequences that it entails. I do not wish to say anything on a personal note, but I want to underline the depth of the tragic consequences for the entire world, because the universal legal order has been destroyed to such a degree that represents the collapse of civilization.

Fortunately, in our time, there are honorable authors who have carved the truth into history so such mistakes would not be repeated and the future generations would know what happened. I am confident that this will happen. In the true history of this era, your *ad hoc* justice will serve as an illustration of monstrous events as one century turned into another. Gentlemen, you cannot imagine what a privilege it is, even under these conditions you have imposed on me, to have truth and justice as my allies.

I am sure that you cannot even conceive this.

Thank you Mr. Robinson. Unfortunately, I did not have the opportunity to present everything that I wished to, but I believe that I will be given this opportunity, unless you deny it to me by some other means.

* * *
* *
*

1 *Robert Badinter*, French scholar and politician, Chairman of the Arbitration Commission established by the European Community in 1991 to arbitrate issues of succession among the republics of the Socialist Federal Republic of Yugoslavia.
2 *JNA*, the Yugoslav People's Army.
3 *HDZ*, the Croatian Democratic Union, the ruling party in Croatia under the leadership of Franjo Tudjman.
4 *SFRY*, the Socialist Federal Republic of Yugoslavia.
5 *Lord Peter Carrington*, formerly British Foreign Secretary, Chairman of the European Community Peace Conference on Yugoslavia 1991-92.
6 *NDH*, the Independent State of Croatia (1941-1945), a satellite of Nazi Germany.
7 President Milosevic is actually referring to Erich Schmidt-Eenboom, former German BND (secret service) agent, who published Der Schattenkreiger, Klaus Kinkel und der BND (The Shadow Warrior: Klaus Kinkel and the BND) (Dusseldorf: ECON, 1995).
8 Cedric Thornberry, Peacekeeping, Peacemaking and Human Rights (Belfast: University of Ulster, 1995).
9 *Jose Cutileiro*, Portuguese diplomat, chaired negotiations on Bosnia-Herzegovina in the European Union Peace Conference that resulted in the Lisbon agreement, which was signed on March 18, 1992, by Alija Izetbegovic, Radovan Karadzic and Mate Boban. It provided for the regional cantonization of the country along ethnic national lines.
10 *General Philippe Morillon*, French commander of UNPROFOR in Bosnia-Herzegovina in 1993.
11 *General Lewis MacKenzie*, Canadian commander of UNPROFOR in Bosnia-Herzegovina in 1992.
12 Lewis MacKenzie, *Peacekeeper: The Road to Sarajevo* (Vancouver: Douglas & McIntyre Ltd, 1993).
13 *Cyrus Vance*, formerly US Secretary of State, United Nations envoy who negotiated the Vance Peace Plan for the Krajina (Croatia) in January 1992. The Plan established a cease-fire and put the region under four UN protected areas (UNPAs). It provided for the withdrawal of the Yugoslav army, the disarming of Serb militia, and the restoration of control of local government, including the police, to population majorities, the Serbs, in the UNPAs.
14 *Madeleine Albright*, US Secretary of State 1997-2000.
15 President Milosevic is actually referring to Jack Kelley, the *USA Today* reporter who was forced to resign after admitting that he fabricated and embellished stories. Mr. Kelley, in a 1999 *USA Today* article, claimed to have seen a document "typed on army stationery and stamped by the Supreme Defense Council of the Yugoslav Army Headquarters in Belgrade, which is headed by Milosevic." The purported document allegedly ordered the ethnic cleansing of Cusk in Kosovo. When it was demonstrated that no such document ever existed, the Tribunal threw out the evidence.
16 *Lord David Owen*, formerly British Foreign Secretary, Co-Chairman of the Steering Committee of the International Conference on the former Yugoslavia 1992-1994.

17 David Owen, *Balkan Odyssey* (New York: Harcourt Brace & Company, 1995).

18 *Javier Perez de Cuellar*, Peruvian diplomat, Secretary General of the United Nations 1982-1991.

19 Austro-German-Italian Triple Alliance formed in May 1882.

20 *Trabant*, German term for satellite

21 *The Tripartite Pact*, an agreement signed by Germany, Italy and Japan on September 27, 1940. The signatories agreed to cooperate with one another in establishing "a new order in Europe and East Asia."

22 *The Cutileiro Plan*, see footnote 9.

23 *KLA*, the Kosovo Liberation Army.

24 *OSCE*, Organization for Security and Cooperation in Europe; formerly CSCE, Conference on Security and Cooperation in Europe.

25 *Kosmet*, the abbreviated designation for Kosovo and Metohija.

26 *Antonio Cassese*, The Right of Peoples to Self-Determination (London: Cambridge University Press, 1995).

27 *The National Liberation Struggle* is the official designation for the Partisan resistance movement in Yugoslavia during World War II led by Josip Broz Tito.

28 The Yugoslav Constitution of 1974 defines Yugoslavia as a country comprised of six constituent nations: Serbs, Croats, Slovenes, Macedonians, Montenegrins and Bosnian Muslims, and nationalities, or national minorities, such as Albanians, Hungarians, Rumanians and others.

29 The United States Senate Policy Committee of the Republican Party, "The Kosovo Liberation Army: Does Clinton Policy Support Group with Terror, Drug Ties? From 'Terrorists' to 'Partners,'" March 31, 1999.

30 *Richard Holbrooke*, Assistant Secretary of State and the US envoy who negotiated the Dayton Accords on Bosnia-Herzegovina in 1995.

31 Wesley K. Clark, *Waging Modern War* (New York: Public Affairs, 2001).

32 Warren Zimmermann, *Origins of a Catastrophe: Yugoslavia and Its Destroyers* (New York: Random House, 1996).

33 *The Vance Plan*, see footnote 13.

34 *Heinrich Himmler*, Chief of the Gestapo 1936-1945; in charge of establishment of concentration camps and extermination of Jews and others 1941-1945.

35 "Iran Gave Bosnia Leader $500,000, CIA Alleges: Classified Report Says Izetbegovic Has Been 'Co-Opted,' Contradicting U.S. Public Assertion of Rift," *Los Angeles Times*, 12/31/96. Ellipses in original. Quoted from United States Senate Republican Policy Committee, "Clinton-Approved Iranian Arms Transfers Help Turn Bosnia into Militant Islamic Base," January 16, 1997.

36 *Patrick Ashdown*, British diplomat, the European Union High Representative for Bosnia-Herzegovina 2002 to the present.

37 The speech President Milosevic gave on June 28, 1989, on the occasion of the commemoration of six-hundred-year anniversary of the Battle of Kosovo.

38 *Robin Cook*, formerly British Minister of Foreign Affairs.

APPENDICES

EXPERTS IN INTERNATIONAL LAW BACK MILOSEVIC DEFENSE

By John Catalinotto

Fifty people interested in the defense of the former Yugoslav president attended an international conference here February 26, 2005 to discuss "The Hague Proceedings against Slobodan Milosevic: Emerging Issues in International Law."

The group was concerned that the International Criminal Tribunal for the former Yugoslavia (ICTY) is attempting to cut short his legal defense.

The meeting brought together top jurists in international law, mainly from Europe and the United States but including a representative from India. The speakers made persuasive presentations exposing the illegitimacy of the ICTY and the case against President Milosevic.

The case has gone through a number of phases since NATO forces kidnapped the Serb leader from prison in Belgrade in June 2001. When the proceedings opened in February 2002, the media dubbed them the "trial of the century." Milosevic and Serbia were to be blamed for 10 years of civil war in the Balkans in the 1990s.

However, Milosevic was able, even with the minimal assistance available to him and despite serious medical problems, to turn the tables on the ICTY during cross-examination and indict the leaders of NATO for 10 years of aggression aimed at destroying Yugoslavia.

The result was that the corporate media stopped reporting on the trial, thus turning it into a de facto secret kangaroo court. Now the prosecution is attempting to limit Milosevic's active defense case and bring the trial to a close as rapidly as possible.

International jurists

Present at the Feb. 26 conference were former U.S. Attorney General Ramsey Clark, former Bulgarian presidential candidate Professor Velko Valkanov, Professor Dr. Hans Köchler of Austria, Professor Aldo Bernardini of Italy, Canadian international attorney Christopher Black, Dr. John Laughland of Britain and Professor Bhim Singh, chair of the Jammu Kashmir National Panther Party. Maitre Tiphaine Dickson of Quebec had to cancel her appearance but submitted a paper read by one of the participants.

Clark, a founding member of the International Action Center, said his visit to Milosevic the day before had showed the "triumph of the human spirit" and called the president "undaunted." Clark said "the violence and deaths of the wars on Yugoslavia were caused by others" and "the real crime was that of organizing the war."

Clark compared the situation in Yugoslavia to that of the U.S. Civil War, although in the Balkans the reactionary side won. "He [Milosevic] was blamed for doing what Abraham Lincoln did in the American Civil War—and that was trying to preserve the Union. Lincoln said many times that his sole purpose was to preserve the Union, yet here the United States' sole purpose was to destroy

Yugoslavia, so that the 'end of history' would appear real," said Clark.

"To do that you had to demonize and destroy the leadership that aimed to preserve the Yugoslav union," he added. "And to have its way the United States had to corrupt the United Nations and international justice."

Professor Valkonov pointed out that with regard to both Serbia and Iraq, "the United States violated all laws" to carry out military attacks on these countries.

Vladimir Krsljanin of the International Committee for the Defense of Slobodan Milosevic announced plans to staff an office in The Hague. Two young activists will help Milosevic prepare his defense case in the remaining time and publicize the results. Krsljanin asked for the necessary financial and organizational support from those who understand the importance of refusing to allow NATO powers to be the sole ones to write the recent history of the Balkans.

ARTISTS' APPEAL FOR MILOSEVIC

For over two years now, Slobodan Milosevic has been on trial before the International Criminal Tribunal for former Yugoslavia - a Security Council institution of dubious legality - charged with 66 counts of war crimes, crimes against humanity and genocide. Over 500,000 pages of documents and 5000 videocassettes have been filed as evidence by the Prosecution. There have been some 300 trial days. More than 300 witnesses have testified. The trial transcript is near 33,000 pages. Yet after all this time and effort, the Prosecution has failed to present significant or compelling evidence of any criminal act or intention of President Milosevic.

In fact, it has been revealed that some prosecution witnesses have been coerced to lie under oath, others have committed perjury. Former NATO commander Wesley Clark, was allowed, in violation of the principle of an open trial, to give testimony in private, with Washington able to apply for removal of any parts of his evidence from the public record they deemed to be against US interests.

President Milosevic was indicted during the 78 day continuous bombardment of Yugoslavia by US-led NATO forces, which used cluster bombs and depleted uranium, attempted to assassinate Milosevic by bombing his residence, killed thousands of civilians and caused billions of dollars of damage to the country's infrastructure. This illegal act of undeclared war is in clear violation of the NATO Charter, the UN Charter, and International Law. Yet neither Wesley Clark, nor the leaders of NATO countries have been indicted for the crimes of which Slobodan Milosevic is accused.

The proceedings of the ICTY against Slobodan Milosevic, as a large and growing number of international jurists has publicly stated, respect neither the principles nor even the appearance of justice. According to Ramsey Clark, the former Attorney-General of the United States, "the spectacle of this huge onslaught by an enormous prosecution support team with vast resources pitted against a single man, defending himself, cut off from all effective assistance, his supporters under attack everywhere and his health slipping away from the constant strain, portrays the essence of unfairness, of persecution". And now that presiding judge Richard May has resigned his position for unspecified health reasons, it appears inevitable, the issue prejudged, that the trial will nevertheless continue, in spite of the virtual impossibility that a new judge will be able to come to grips with the mountain of evidence presented so far.

If justice is not just, if prosecution is persecution, if international law is flouted in order to "enforce international law", we are indeed now living in the dystopian world of George Orwell's 1984. The neighborhood bully has decided the world is his back yard. The implications of this egregious use of "power politics" go beyond the unjust trial of Slobodan Milosevic: the "new world order" now being implemented is simply inhuman and intolerable. What can be done to change this cruel and criminal state of affairs?

Let us remember that it was not long ago that 15 million people marched on the same day in a gesture of international solidarity to say no to the Bush junta's illegal war on Iraq. Now is the time for another such gesture. For if this trial continues, the only triumphs will be those of travesty over justice, power over principle, disinformation over truth. And many feel that the sum total of these acts constitutes state terrorism perpetrated on a virtually defenseless country and its legally elected president.

As artists, our work is to broaden our horizons, to become more human and to share that humanity. And to create. Destruction is intolerable to us. It is intolerable that courts be used to justify the killing of civilians, the destruction of a sovereign nation, and the demonization and imprisonment of that nation's leader. Let us now create a massive demonstration of our humanity. Now is the time to make ourselves heard loud and clear, once again, by publicly denouncing this injustice. We urge you to join your efforts to those of the International Committee for the Defense of Slobodan Milosevic.

March-April 2004

Montreal-New York-Moscow-Paris

SIGNED:

Robert Dickson, poet (winner of the Governor General's award for French poetry 2002), Canada

Harold Pinter, playwright, UK (winner of Nobel Prize for Literature 2005)

Peter Handke, writer, Austria/France

Alexander Zinoviev, writer, philosopher, Russian Federation

Valeri Ganichev, writer (President of the Writers' Union of Russia), Russian Federation

Vyacheslav Klykov, sculptor (President of the International Fund for Slavonic Literacy and Culture), Russian Federation

Dimitri Analis, poet, Greece/France

Valentin Rasputin, novelist, Russian Federation

Fulvio Grimaldi, filmmaker, journalist, Italy

Vladimir Kostrov, poet (winner of Tyutchev and Bunin awards), Russian Federation

Nadja Tesich, novelist, Yugoslavia/US

Rolf Becker, actor, Germany

Milos Raickovich, composer, Yugoslavia/US

Alan Mandell, theatre artist, US

Mick Collins, theatre artist, US/France

John Steppling, screenwriter, playwright, US/Poland

Joseph Goodrich, playwright, US

Godfred Louis-Jensen, architect, Denmark

David Morgan, poet, Canada

Larissa Kritskaya, composer, journalist, Russia/USA

Katarina Kostic, poet, writer, Canada

Paolo Teobaldelli, writer, philosopher, Italy

Cédéric Michaud, photographe, Nouvel-Ontario, Canada

Nikolai Petev, writer (President of the Writers' Union of Bulgaria), Bulgaria
For a full listing of all signers and other information on artists appeal see: www.icdsm.org

IMPOSITION OF COUNSEL ON SLOBODAN MILOSEVIC THREATENS THE FUTURE OF INTERNATIONAL LAW AND THE LIFE OF THE DEFENDANT

H.E. Mr. KOFI ANNAN, Secretary General of the United Nations,

H.E. Mr. JULIAN ROBERT HUNTE, President of 58th Session of the UN General Assembly

Romanian (Russian) Presidency of the UN Security Council,

To all members of the UN Security Council, to all members of the UN

Cc: International Criminal Tribunal for the former Yugoslavia

We the undersigned, jurists, law professors, and international criminal lawyers, hereby declare our alarm and concern that the International Criminal Tribunal for the Former Yugoslavia (ICTY) is preparing the imposition of counsel upon an unwilling accused, Slobodan Milosevic.

This apparently punitive measure is contrary to international law, incompatible with the adversarial system of criminal justice adopted by the Security Council in Resolution 808, and ignores the court's obligation to provide adequate medical care and provisional release to the defendant. The ICTY, instead of taking appropriate measures to alleviate Slobodan Milosevic's long-standing medical problems, has compounded them. The ICTY has ignored repeated requests for provisional release, to which everyone presumed innocent is entitled, has imposed unrealistically short preparation periods on the defense, and has permitted the introduction of an inordinate quantity of Prosecution evidence, much of which was bereft of probative value, thereby increasing Mr. Milosevic's level of stress, the principal trigger of his illness. Chamber III has been informed of this by their chosen cardiologist. The defendant has been denied examination by his own physician, a further violation of his rights.

Now, having brought about the very degradation of President Milosevic's health of which it had been warned, the ICTY seeks to impose counsel upon him over his objections, rather than granting him provisional release in order to receive adequate and proper medical care, a reasonable measure reflected in domestic and international law and practice. The envisaged imposition of counsel constitutes an egregious violation of internationally recognized judicial rights, and will serve only to aggravate Mr Milosevic's life-threatening illness and further discredit these proceedings.

The right to defend one's self against criminal charges is central in both international law and in the very structure of the adversarial system. The fundamental, minimum rights provided to a defendant under the Rome Statute of the International Criminal Court, as well as the under the Statutes of the International Criminal Tribunals for Rwanda and Yugoslavia, include the right to defend oneself in person. The general economy of these provisions all envisage the reality that rights are afforded to an accused, not to a lawyer. The right afforded is to represent oneself against charges brought by the Prosecution and subsidiary to this, to receive the assistance of counsel, if an accused expresses the wish to receive such assistance. However, if, as Slobodan Milosevic, a defendant unequivocally expresses his objection to representation by counsel, his right to represent himself supercedes a court's or prosecutor's preference for assigning defense counsel. As stated by the U.S. Supreme Court, with respect to the Sixth Amendment of the Bill of Rights, which bears a striking similarity to Article 21 of the ICTY Statute:

> "It speaks of the 'assistance' of counsel, and an assistant, however expert, is still an assistant. The language and spirit of the Sixth Amendment contemplate that counsel, like the other defense tools guaranteed by the Amendment, shall be an aid to a willing defendant — not an organ of the State interposed between an unwilling defendant and his right to defend himself personally. To thrust counsel upon the accused, against his considered wish, thus violates the logic of the Amendment. In such a case, counsel is not an assistant, but a master; and the right to make a defense is stripped of the personal character upon which the Amendment insists."

Faretta v.California, 422 U.S. 806 (1975)

The ICTY Statute (as well as ICTR and ICC Statutes) similarly grant "defense tools," such as the right to be represented by counsel, or the right for counsel to be provided free of charge, if the accused is indigent. The essence of the right to represent oneself is defeated when the right to counsel becomes an obligation. As stated in Farretta, supra:

> "An unwanted counsel 'represents' the defendant only through a tenuous and unacceptable legal fiction. Unless the accused has acquiesced in such representation, the defense presented is not the defense guaranteed him by the Constitution, for, in a very real sense, it is not his defense."

Id.

Nor would the defense of Slobodan Milosevic be the defense guaranteed him under international law, were he to have counsel imposed upon him against his will.

The ICTY's general structure is that of an adversarial system of criminal justice. Other legal influences have been integrated to the Rules of Procedure and Evidence, but the nature of the proceedings, which involve a prosecutor and defendant, as parties, presenting evidence before a panel whose function is that of arbiter, is unquestionably of an adversarial nature. In the adversarial system, history has eloquently illustrated that imposition of counsel on an unwilling accused is the practice of political courts, and does not have its place in a democratic system of justice, much less before an institution that will generate precedent for a truly legitimate international criminal jurisdiction, whose establishment has been the fruit of half a century of struggle:

> In the long history of British criminal jurisprudence, there was only one tribunal that ever adopted a practice of forcing counsel upon an unwilling defendant in a criminal proceeding. The tribunal was the Star Chamber. That curious institution, which flourished in the late 16th and early 17th centuries, was of mixed executive and judicial character, and characteristically departed from common-law traditions. For those reasons, and because it specialized in trying 'political' offenses, the Star Chamber has for centuries symbolized disregard of basic individual rights.
>
> Faretta, Id.

Recently, the ICTY has ordered the Prosecutor, and only the Prosecutor, to provide an opinion with respect to the imposition of counsel in the absence of instructions or cooperation from Mr. Milosevic. The Chamber has repeatedly referred to its obligation to carry out a fair trial, and held, when it acknowledged the right to self-representation in April 2003, that it "has indeed an obligation to ensure that a trial is fair and expeditious; moreover, where the health of the Accused is in issue, that obligation takes on special significance." Article 21 of the ICTY's Statute states that the Chamber must exercise this obligation "with full respect for the rights of the accused." However, expediency has become, as the defendant is set to present essential and potentially embarrassing evidence, the Chamber's apparently overwhelming concern.

Imposition of counsel, even "standby counsel", as appears to be presently envisaged by the ICTY, will not alleviate any of the difficulties facing the process: it will not treat, much less cure, Slobodan Milosevic's malignant hypertension; it will not provide the defendant with the time and conditions to prepare his case; it will not redress the gross imbalance in the resources accorded the Prosecutor and the defense, a redress required by the principle of equality of arms, which the Court professes to recognize. If counsel is imposed, Slobodan Milosevic's basic right to represent himself will be violated, and he will still have only 150 days to present his defense, only half of the time allotted to the Prosecution.

It is presently unclear what role an imposed counsel would play. Whatever it may be, it is certain that there is no benefit to be gained from going forward with this unprecedented measure. The ICTY Statute provides the minimum right to be present for one's trial. If Slobodan Milosevic's medical condition does not permit him to attend the proceedings, and he does not waive his right to be present, the ICTY does not have the jurisdiction to hold hearings in his absence. Adjournments will continue as long as measures are not taken to treat Mr. Milosevic's malignant hypertension, a condition that cannot be treated by further violating his rights, threatening to remove him from the process, or by transferring his defense to a complete stranger.

The ICTY assigned three counsel to act as amicus curiae, and whose stated role is to ensure, *inter alia*, a fair trial. It is doubtful an imposed counsel, even a "standby counsel" could provide any additional assistance, without hijacking President Milosevic's defense, or simply silencing him. Furthermore, any reference to precedent with respect to the imposition of standby counsel is inapposite. In the case of Dr Seselj, "standby counsel" has been imposed, before the beginning of a trial, and to prevent "disruption" of the proceedings.

President Slobodan Milosevic does not recognize the ICTY. He asserts his innocence, and steadfastly criticizes the ICTY and NATO. He is innocent until proven otherwise, and has every right to oppose the legitimacy of this institution. By imposing counsel, the ICTY would not only violate his right to self-representation, but his right to present relevant evidence demonstrating the repeated violations of Yugoslavia's sovereignty over a decade. These violations led to NATO's illegal war of aggression against and bombing of Yugoslavia — at the very height of which an indictment against Slobodan Milosevic was confirmed by the ICTY

— in a transparent bid to deprive the Yugoslav people of a voice to negotiate peace and in order to justify the continuation of that war of aggression.

The trial of Slobodan Milosevic before the ICTY has been adjourned until August 31st, 2004. The Prosecutor has presented 295 witnesses in as many days, all of which have been cross-examined by the defendant in person, as he does not recognize the ICTY as a judicial body, and signals this non-recognition by refusing to assign counsel. Slobodan Milosevic is a law school graduate, was three times elected to the highest state offices of Serbia and Yugoslavia, and has by all accounts ably contested the Prosecution's case. There is no question as to his mental fitness and ability to waive his right to counsel. The ICTY may not enjoy President Milosevic's criticism. Nonetheless, the public benefits of respecting his right to self-representation far outweigh whatever embarrassment might be visited upon the ICTY. Justice demands that Slobodan Milosevic be given the right to demonstrate that the Security Council institution detaining him is a political weapon against the sovereignty and self-determination of the people of Serbia and all the peoples of Yugoslavia.

Nelson Mandela represented himself during the infamous Rivonia trials of the 1960s. Mandela mounted a political defense against apartheid, yet even the South African judiciary did not impose counsel to silence him. The ICTY is poised to threaten the future of international law by doing what even apartheid-era judges dared not do — gag a defendant and impair his ability to respond to a case. A case, we note, made unwieldy, unintelligible and inexplicably lengthy by the Prosecutor, with the Chamber's assent, and not by Slobodan Milosevic. Indeed, most observers of the process have noted that the Prosecutor failed to present compelling evidence to support any of their charges; rather than stay the proceedings, the ICTY permitted the Prosecutor to present additional witnesses, in apparent desperation to make something stick.

The right to defend oneself in person is at the heart of the International Covenant for Civil and Political Rights. The United Nations should not tolerate these continuing violations of international law in the name of expediency. Using a detained person's inappropriately treated illness as an excuse to infringe upon his rights and silence him, and embark upon a "radical reform" of the proceedings— as the Chamber is now considering, by changing the rules in mid-trial, and to the defendant's detriment— is a perversion of both the letter and spirit of international law.

As jurists, we are deeply concerned that the planned imposition of counsel constitutes an irrevocable precedent, and potentially deprives any accused person of the right to present a meaningful defense in the future. In the case of Slobodan Milosevic, this measure will only increase his hypertension and place his life at risk.

The ICTY and Security Council will be held responsible for the tragically predictable consequences of their actions.

July 29, 2004

Signed by 58 lawyers, 38 University professors of Law and 16 other legal or juridical experts and professionals from 18 countries.

For a full listing of signers see: www.icdsm.org

Index

1974 Constitution 62-63
1990 Constitution 64

Abdel-Rahman, Sheikh Omar 93
Accounting for Genocide 45
Afghanistan 23, 67, 72-73, 77
al Qaeda 50, 68, 72-73, 76-77, 92
Albania 61-64, 66-67, 76, 81-82
Albanian demonstrations 48
Albanian Labor Party 62
Albanian secessionists 48, 64
Albanian separatists 49, 62-63
Albanian terrorists 24, 49, 52, 57, 64, 73, 78-79
Albright, Madeleine 74-75, 82, 105
al-Husseini, Amin 91
Allen, Richard 46
Andrassy, Prime Minister 37
Army of the Republika Srpska 95
Ashdown, Paddy 99
Au Courant 35
Austria-Hungary 36-39, 44
Austro-Hungarian Empire 40
Avramov, Smilja 46, 48

Babic, Milan 89
Badinter, Robert 105
Bajramovic, Miro 87
Baker, James 51
Balists 61
Balkan Odyssey 86, 106
Balkan route 67
Balkan Tragedy 87
Balkans 36, 38, 43, 47, 49-50, 60, 66
Barani, Halid 57
Baranja 86
Baric 81
Bedjaoui, Mohammed 29
Belgrade 21, 28, 32, 47, 66, 70-73, 78, 80, 82, 95, 103, 105
Berchtold, Count 38
Berlin 50, 61, 64
Berlin memorandum 37
Bernstein, Carl 46
Bigler, Colonel 48
bin Laden, Osama 76-77, 82, 93
Bismarck, Chancellor 37
"Black Legion," 21
Bojkovac, Josip 26
Bosnia 66, 68, 70, 76, 84-86, 89-96, 98, 103, 105-106
Bosnia-Herzegovina 22-23, 26, 30, 49, 52-55, 58, 66, 68, 85-86, 89-95, 103, 105-106
Boston 67
Brioni 24
Brzezinski, Zbigniew 46
Buja, Shukri 57
Burnei 92
Burnham, Erich Schmidt (*see* Schmidt-Eenboom, Erik) 26
Butros-Ghali, Boutros 95
Cassese, Antonio 55, 106
Catholic Church 44-45, 47-48
Ceku, Agim 72
Central Committee of the Soviet Communist Party 61
Central Europe 40-41, 51
Chapel, Derek 78
Chinese Embassy 80
Christopher, Warren 34
Churchill, Winston 42
CIA 23, 69-70, 93, 106
Ciluffo, Frank 67
Clark, General Wesley 70, 74-75, 82, 103, 106
Clinton, William J. 42, 48, 50, 79, 82, 92, 106
Clinton Administration 66-70, 73, 75, 87, 97, 102
Coalition for International Justice 30
Cold War 27, 49
Committee for Foreign Relations 70
Communists 46, 86
Congress of Berlin 61
Convention for the Prevention and Punishment of Genocide 28
Cook, Robin 106
Cooper, Leo 20
Cram, George 20
Croatia 19-21, 23, 25-27, 32-34, 36, 43-45, 47-48, 50-56, 58, 64, 66, 72, 83-89, 91, 95-96, 102-103, 105
Croatian Parliament 43
Cuellar, Perez de 33, 106
Cutileiro Jose 50, 94, 105-106
Czechoslovakia 42

Dalmatia 40, 86-87
Danke Deutschland 44

Danube 80, 88
Daruvar 22
Decani 72
del Vallo, Cardinal Mario 44
Demaci, Adem 62
Democratic National Convention 67
deni de justice 29
Deronjic, Miroslav 99
Deutsche Zeitung 34
Die Welt 34
Die Zeit 35
Diktat 18, 51
Dimitrov case 103
Djuflaj, Sadik 72
Djuflaj, Valon 72
Dnevnik 86
Drang nach Osten 44
Drecun, Milovan 71
Dreyfus case 103
Drina River 21
Drost, Peter 20
Dubai 92
Dumas, Roland 34
Dusan, Emperor 79

Eastern Bloc 49
Eastern Europe 47, 51, 80
Economist 100
El Salvador 69
Elich, Gregory 87
Encyclopedia of the Holocaust, McMillan's 45
Erdemovic, Drazen 88, 99
ethnic cleansing 47, 58, 60, 77, 89, 97, 102, 105
Europe 67, 74-75, 77-78, 80-81, 92-93, 102, 106
European 64, 89, 91, 105-106
European Community 18-20, 24, 26-27, 33-34, 50-52, 105

Federation of American Scientists 66
Fein, Professor Helen 45
Fellner, Peter von 95
Feral Tribune 88
Financial Times 79
First World War 32
Foreign Affairs 19
France 25, 31, 39, 46, 82
Frankfurter Allgemeine Zeitung 35
Freedom Fighters 70
Frlec, Boris 33

Gallois, General Pierre-Marie 35
Gazimestan 100
Gelbard, Richard 66, 69
Geneva Conventions 28
genocide 20-21, 28, 43, 45, 72, 76, 84, 86, 103
Genocide in Satellite Croatia 1941-1945 45
Genscher, Hans-Dietrich 25-26, 30-31, 33, 35, 41-42, 44
German, Patriarch 59
Germany 18-19, 21, 23, 25-26, 28, 31-36, 38-45, 50-52, 54, 64, 89, 91, 105-106
Gertz, Ted 20
Globalized Organized Crime Program 67
Globus 86
Goebbels, Josef 43
Golden Crescent 67
Gorbachev, Michael 47
Gorchakov, Prince 37
Gospels 48
Gospic 88
Great Britain 31, 39, 45
Greater Serbia 36-38, 40, 42, 81
Grey, Sir Edward 39
Guskova, Professor Elena 60-61

Habsburg monarchy 40
Habsburg rule 37
Haig, Alexander 46
Handzar Division 25, 91
Haradinaj, Ramus and Daut 72
Hartman, Ralf 36,, 38, 43
HDZ 22, 84-85, 105
Hedges, Chris 88
Helsinki 51
Helsinki Final Act 24
Herljevic, Franjo 62
heroin 67
Hezbollah 23, 50
Hiroshima. 23
Hitler, Adolph 24, 26, 42-44, 47, 82, 85, 91
Holbrooke, Richard 69, 82, 106
holocaust 42, 45, 87
Holy See 25-26, 44, 46-47
holy warriors 23, 92
Horowitz, Donald 24
Horowitz, Louis 20
Hoxha, Enver 61, 63
humanitarian intervention 47

Identitet 88
Independent State of Croatia 83-86, 91, 105

International Community 18, 27-28, 30, 50, 52-53, 70, 72, 78
International Court of Justice 29, 56
International Criminal Court 54
international law 24-25, 27, 39, 52, 54-55, 82, 94
International Monetary Fund 18
Iran 92-93, 106
Iranian Revolutionary Guards 92
Islam Between East and West 22
Islamic Declaration, The 22, 91
Islamic fundamentalists 24, 49, 52-53, 91
Istanbul 37
Izetbegovic, Alija 22-23, 50, 90-94, 98, 105-106

Jagow, Gottlieb von 38
Jankovac 22
Jeddah 23
Jews 43, 91, 106
jihad 91-92
Jiricek, Konstantin 58
JNA 20-21, 23, 32-33, 54, 83, 88, 94, 105
Jovic, Borislav 55
judi inclusa sua 29

Kadijevic, Veljko 84
Karadzic, Radovan 99, 105
Kardelj, Edvard 84
Kenya 82
KFOR 79
Kingdom of the Serbs, Croats and Slovenes 39, 47
Kinkel, Klaus 26, 30, 35-36, 41-42, 79, 105
KLA 31, 50, 57, 64-73, 75-77, 82, 106
Kljujic 98
Koha Ditore 31
Kohl, Helmut 26, 31-32, 34, 36, 79
Kolsek, Konrad 20
KonKret 64
Kosmet 53, 57, 59-60, 62-63, 73, 77-79, 81, 106
Kosovo 17, 19, 23, 27-28, 30-31, 48-50, 52-53, 56-64, 66-81, 91, 96, 100-101, 103, 105-106
Kosovo and Metohija 61-63, 67-70, 72-73, 80-81, 91, 96, 106
Kosovo Protection Corps 71-72
Kosydowski, Michael 70
Krajina 21, 48-49, 54, 84, 86-87, 98, 105
Kristallnacht 77, 88
Kristan, Ivan 60, 61, 63

Krnjevic-Miskovic, Damjan de 77
Kroja, Mustafa 59

La Stampa 47
Lazarevic, General 96
League of Nations 18
Lebanon 23
Levar, Milan 88
Liberal Party 41-42
Ljeviska, Holy Mother of 79
Ljubljana 33, 48
Loncar, Budimir 19
London Treaty 40
Lubbers, Rudd 34
Lucani 81
Lukic, General 96
Lyndaker, Leo 48

Macedonia 49, 55, 57, 66, 74, 91
MacKenzie, General Lewis 76-78, 105
Makarije, Prior 59
Malaysia 92
Malovic, Josip 26
Markale Market 70
Markovic, Ante 19-20
Martic, Milan 98
Maspok movement 83
mass graves 76, 84
McGee, Marcus 30
Medak Pocket 72, 89
Mercep, Tomislav 87
Mesic, Stjepan 19, 26, 35, 43-44
MI5 65
MI6 65
Milady, Thomas Patrick 25
Milan, Prince 37
Miljevacki Plateau 89
Mitteleuropa 40
Mladic, Ratko 98
Montenegro 23, 102
Morava 80
Morillon, General Philippe 98, 105
Morocco 23, 91
MPRI 49
mujahedin 22-23, 92
My Confidential Conversations with Hitler 82

narco Mafia 19, 23, 64
Nasi Dani 93
National Interest 77
NATO 21, 23, 28, 30-31, 48-50, 52-54, 61, 67-68, 70-71, 73-82, 102-103

Naumann, Friedrich 40-42, 51, 74
Nazis 23-25, 45, 49, 52, 58-59, 61, 85, 105
NDH 25, 105
Nerval Group 85
Neubacher, Herman 59
NGOs 30
Nicaragua 69
Norshchinskaya, Natalia 78
North America 77
Novi Sad 81, 86
Nuremberg 18, 52, 54

Oblakovac 22
Ogledalo 78
Ojdanic, General 74, 96
Operation Storm 47, 72
Operations Flash and Storm 47, 89, 97
Opus Dei 46, 48
Organization for Security and Cooperation in Europe 18, 106
Organization of the Islamic Conference 22
Origins of a Catastrophe 85, 106
Orijaca 22
Orthodox churches 79
OSCE 50, 64, 70, 106
Osijek 88
Ottoman Empire 86
Owen, Lord David 33-34, 47, 50, 86-89, 93, 105-106

Pakistan 23, 67, 91-92
Pancevo 81
Papuk 22
Paris 24, 33
Paris, Edmond 45
Patriotic League Day 93
Pavelic, Ante 43, 45, 91
Pavkovic, General 96
Perucica 89
Pike, John 66
Pittsburgh 48
Plato 79
Podravska Slatina 22
Politics International 26
Pope 25-26, 35, 44-48
John Paul II, Pope 25, 35, 44, 47
Princip, Gavrilo 38
Pristina 31, 63

Racak 70-71
Rambouillet 69-70, 75
Raska 23

Rauschning, Herman 82
Riyadh 92
Roma 65, 102
Rome 33, 51
Rugova, Ibrahim 65

Sandzak 23
Sarajevo 23, 38, 42, 47, 91-92, 105
satellite state 41
Saudi Arabia 66, 82, 92
Sava 80
Schmidt-Eenboom, Erich 105
SDA 90, 93
Security Council 67-68, 72, 95
self-determination 54-55, 94, 106
September 11, 2001 50
Serbia 23, 25, 28, 36-42, 44, 47-48, 52-53, 57-58, 62-65, 72, 76, 78-82, 84, 89-90, 96-98, 100-103
"Serbian chauvinists" 43
Serbien muss sterben 41
SFRY 24, 53-55, 60, 83, 105
Shea, Jamie 31
Skenderbeg Division 91
Slatina 22
Slavonia 22, 40, 86-87, 89
Slavonska Pozega 22
Slovenia 19-21, 25-27, 32-34, 47-48, 50-51, 53-55, 64, 83
Slunj 22
Smithson declaration 25
Socialist Federal Republic of Yugoslavia 27, 49, 54, 105
Soros, George 30-31, 82
Soros Foundation 30-31
South Slav question 38
South Slavs 37-38, 42
Soviet Union 31, 51
Spegelj, Martin 86
Srebrenica 48, 88, 98-99
State Duma of Russia 78
Stedman, John 19
Svinjarevo 22

Taci, Hasim 67
Tanzania 82
Slavenko Terzic 59
The Florida Times-Union Daily 78
The Globe and Mail 30
The Hague 71, 78-79, 88
The History of the Yugoslav Crisis from 1990 to 2000 60

The Honorable Mediators 36
The Independent 84, 100, 105
The National Post 76
The New World Order and the Security Council: Testing the Legality of Its Acts 30
The New York Times 30, 82, 86, 88
The Scotsman 65
The Second Battle of Kosovo 71
The Wall Street Journal 77
The Washington Post 30, 72
Thornberry, Cedric 27, 105
Time magazine 100
Tjednik 88
Tokyo 54
Trabant 106
Tribunal 17-19, 27-31, 39, 46, 52, 79, 105
Tripartite Pact 42, 106
Triple Alliance 38, 106
Tudjman, Franjo 21, 23, 26, 53, 55, 84-88, 105
Turkey 64, 92
Turkish rule 37

U.S. Congress 30, 67, 70, 93
U.S. House of Representatives 67
ultimatum 24, 39, 75
UN Charter 19, 27, 29
UN protected zones 48
UN Security Council Resolution 1160 68
UN Security Council Resolution 1199 68
UN Security Council Resolution 1203 68
UN Security Council Resolution 1244 72, 81
United Nations 18, 25, 27, 31, 53, 57, 67, 76-77, 95, 105-106
United States 18, 24-25, 31, 33, 45-49, 51, 67, 106
United States Congress 49
UNPROFOR 27, 76, 105
USA 27-28, 34, 39, 42, 45, 49-54, 64, 66, 82, 93, 105
USA Today 34, 105
USSR 42, 45
US State Department 66
Ustasha 20-21, 24, 26, 45, 47, 52, 84-85, 87

Vance, Cyrus 27, 50, 89, 105-106
Vasiljevic, General 96
Vatican 18-19, 23, 25-28, 34, 44-48, 50, 52, 54

Verification Mission 70-71, 74
Versailles Peace Treaty 61
Vienna 37-38, 44, 86
VNOS 97
Vojvodina 64
Vukovar 88
"Vukovar Wolves," 21

Walker, William 69-70
Wehrmacht 43
Western Slavonia 22, 87, 89
Woodward, Susan 87
World Bank 18
World Trade Center 93
World War I 40, 42, 44, 47, 59
World War II 23, 25, 32, 40, 44-47, 58-59, 61-62, 83-84, 86, 106

Yalta 46
Young Bosnia 38
Young Muslims 90, 92
Yugoslav idea 37
Yugoslav People's Army 20, 32, 105
Yugoslavia 17-20, 23-28, 30, 32-37, 39-40, 42-44, 47-56, 61-64, 66, 68, 73-75, 79-80, 82-85, 87, 89-90, 94-96, 98, 100, 102-103, 105-106

Zagreb 21, 23, 33, 47-48, 84, 86
"Zebra," 21
Zemunik 89
Zimmermann, Warren 83, 85, 94, 106
Zulfikarpasic, Izet Adil 90-91

Hidden Agenda
U.S./NATO Takeover of YugoSlavia

A well researched and documented anthology exposing the illegal roots and procedures of the International Criminal Tribunal for the Former Yugoslavia. Its effort to stage a show trial of Yugoslav President Slobodan Milosevic, is an attempt to find the entire Serb and Yugoslav people guilty of resistance to NATO.

Using evidence presented to dozens of popular international tribunal hearings, it turns the tables on NATO by exposing and demonstrating the war crimes of Milosevic's accusers, including their decade-long conspiracy to wage war on Yugoslavia.

Chapters by Yugoslav President Slobodon Milosevic, former U. S. Attorney General Ramsey Clark, Mumia Abu-Jamal, Michel Chossudovsky, Sara Flounders, Gloria La Riva, Michael Parenti, John Catalinotto, Michael Ratner, Michel Collon and other leading anti-war activists and analysts.(2002)

400 pages, pictures, maps, chronology, index Softcover $19.95

THE DEFENSE SPEAKS: FOR HISTORY AND THE FUTURE
&
HIDDEN AGENDA: U.S./NATO TAKEOVER OF YUGOSLAVIA
are available from

International Action Center
39 W. 14th St. Room 206,New York, NY 10011
212.633.6646

For On-line credit card orders contact:
> *www.LeftBooks.com*

For university, bookstore and library orders contact:
> Independent Publishers Group
> *www.ipgBook.com*